Problem Solving in Primary Mathematics

Problem Solving in Primary Mathematics is an essential text designed to support new and experienced teachers in guiding pupils through mathematical investigations and problem solving, offering a framework that children themselves can begin to adopt as they progress to greater metacognitive awareness.

Underpinned by the latest international research and theory, it examines how individual pupils think and act differently and offers guidance on how to promote independence and autonomy in the classroom. It examines key topics such as:

- Preparing for mathematical learning
- Designing learning material
- Assessing and evaluating learning
- Identifying key points for intervention
- What to do when learning is stalled
- Critical numeracy for real-world problem solving
- Mental Model Theory and the Mental Model Mode
- Different approaches to problem solving and investigating

Aimed at new and experienced educators, particularly those with a maths specialism, and illustrated with investigations and activities, *Problem Solving in Primary Mathematics* demonstrates how frameworks can be used in key mathematical areas and assists students in progressing towards more meaningful problem solving.

Christine Edwards-Leis is Senior Lecturer in Primary Mathematics at St Mary's University, Twickenham, UK. Previously she was lecturer and researcher at University of South Australia. Her research interests are Mental Model Theory and how children use problem-solving strategies in mathematics and design and technology.

Debbie Robinson is Head of Primary Mathematics and Senior Lecturer in Primary Mathematics at St Mary's University, Twickenham, UK. She has extensive experience as both a classroom teacher and advisory teacher in both Primary and Secondary schools. She provided INSET for qualified teachers for BEAM Publications and Education Authorities and her research interests are the use of practical activities, contexts and images to engage learners in mathematics.

Problem Solving in Primary Mathematics

Learning to Investigate!

Christine Edwards-Leis
and Debbie Robinson

LONDON AND NEW YORK

First published 2019
by Routledge
2 Park Square, Milton Park, Abingdon, Oxon OX14 4RN

and by Routledge
711 Third Avenue, New York, NY 10017

Routledge is an imprint of the Taylor & Francis Group, an informa business

© 2019 Christine Edwards-Leis and Debbie Robinson

The right of Christine Edwards-Leis and Debbie Robinson to be identified as authors of this work has been asserted by them in accordance with sections 77 and 78 of the Copyright, Designs and Patents Act 1988.

All rights reserved. No part of this book may be reprinted or reproduced or utilised in any form or by any electronic, mechanical, or other means, now known or hereafter invented, including photocopying and recording, or in any information storage or retrieval system, without permission in writing from the publishers.

Trademark notice: Product or corporate names may be trademarks or registered trademarks, and are used only for identification and explanation without intent to infringe.

British Library Cataloguing-in-Publication Data
A catalogue record for this book is available from the British Library

Library of Congress Cataloging-in-Publication Data
Names: Edwards-Leis, Christine, author.
Title: Problem solving in mathematics / Christine Edwards-Leis.
Description: Abingdon, Oxon ; New York, NY : Routledge, 2018. |
    Includes bibliographical references and index.
Identifiers: LCCN 2018005622 | ISBN 9781138911109 (hbk) |
    ISBN 9781138911116 (pbk) | ISBN 9781315692999 (ebk)
Subjects: LCSH: Mathematics—Study and teaching. | Problem solving. |
    Mathematics teachers—Training of.
Classification: LCC QA11.2. E385 2018 | DDC 372.7/044—dc23
LC record available at https://lccn.loc.gov/2018005622

ISBN: 978-1-138-91110-9 (hbk)
ISBN: 978-1-138-91111-6 (pbk)
ISBN: 978-1-315-69299-9 (ebk)

Typeset in Optima
by Apex CoVantage, LLC

Contents

	Introduction	1
1	Understanding thinking: mental models and why they are relevant to classrooms	5
2	The functions of thinking	19
3	Ways to problem solve and investigate: scaffolds and structures	41
4	Number strings	61
5	Squaring up to the problem	75
6	Rich tasks and big questions	89
7	Changing times	105
8	Problem solving and investigating	121
	Appendix 1: Assessment strategy for PGCE student teachers	129
	Appendix 2: 4R approach to collaboration	131
	Appendix 3: Teacher's notes for squaring up to the problem	135
	Index	137

v

Introduction

Welcome to *Problem Solving in Primary Mathematics: Learning to Investigate!* This text represents for us, the authors, a lifelong relationship with learning, teaching, designing and researching mathematics. When we first started working together at a London higher education institution that provided Primary teacher education courses, we realized that we shared similar approaches to working with student teachers but methods that came from different perspectives. Debbie designed experiential, socially constructed, challenging workshops for student teachers that involved multiple self-made resources and activities; Chris designed similarly engaging sessions but ones that challenged students to consider the conceptual foci for learning. We often worked together with groups and cohorts and have recently reflected that those teaching years were the best we can remember.

The idea for this text emerged from our shared belief that mathematics is necessary for humans to flourish. In an increasingly complex world driven by capitalist ideology, it is imperative that humans understand how they can be positioned by numbers: critical numeracy skills are essential so humans are able to flourish economically. In a world in which rapidly changing technologies are infiltrating the fabric of our lives a conceptual understanding of algorithms is essential so that we can not only participate in life but understand how those very lives are to be governed and monitored. In a world in which Hargreaves (2003) suggested we would be inclined to amuse ourselves to death using computer technology increasingly on hand-held devices, we believe it is essential that we learn to be playful and successful with more diverse types of numerical, spatial and measurement challenges so that we can retain our capacity to problem solve better and communicate our ideas more clearly.

In the coming chapters we talk about Jenny, a child who participated in a research project about mental models of robotics, who while scoring very highly on standardized tests in mathematics had little in her armoury for effective problem solving. Something is missing in how we 'rate' or 'evaluate' mathematical competence

Introduction

if a child who can score well in pen-and-pencil tests but fail to solve 'real-world' problems is seen as a 'high achiever' in mathematics. Jenny was unable to 'problem solve' effectively in a challenge that had only two avenues to explore in order to find a solution; her unwillingness to fail in an attempt to pursue one avenue and her inability to apply a learned problem-solving skill set in the other meant she was left with no option than to ignore the error and proceed as if nothing had gone wrong. We have seen other struggles with mathematical problems and investigations in the student cohorts we have taught at university. The significance of their passing through our course and commencing teaching while lacking the confidence to teach mathematics is what has motivated us to write this book. Like Jenny, no human should miss out on the chance to experience the joy of playing with and being successful at mathematics. We trust that this text will show ways that you can design challenging yet supportive environments for your students while enabling you to understand better the idiosyncratic ways that they will engage with the exciting adventures you plan.

The text opens with an exploration of Mental Model Theory, which is aimed at supporting your approach to understanding how and why each child will interact differently with a learning challenge. Chapter 2 looks at the functions of thinking and how they support reasoning. Reasoning is a significant feature of the national curriculum in England and Wales (Department for Education, 2013), so gaining a comprehensive understanding of what this means in mathematics is key for you to design an environment in which you can confidently facilitate investigations and problem-solving activities. We also introduce the Mental Model Mode, which is a theoretical construct designed to help you understand how the functions of thinking interact; a typology of prompts is provided in Chapter 3 to help you ask questions/prompt pupils as they engage in challenges. Chapter 3 also explains different approaches to problem solving including *bolt-on* and *built-in* approaches. Such ideas will help you design activities that are purposeful and manageable.

Managing how you prepare for mathematical learning is essential, and the time available for this will often govern what you aim to achieve in your classroom. Chapter 3 also explains in detail how to start with neat (focused) types of investigations only to facilitate them to open up into more messy or open-ended events. We also explain how broad or messy types of problem-solving activities that you design can result in quite closed or neat solutions. The structures provided encourage you to look at problem solving and investigating in more broad and informative terms rather than simply as a skill set or acronym to follow. The focus is on the process and the types of activities that the children will enact in order to find one or many solutions.

The remaining, Chapters 4 to 7, explore four ideas in detail. They explain how to set up the activities, how to organize the children, design the learning material and evaluate learning. For each activity we provide ways for you to enable, engage and evaluate the children so that they, like you, can become risk takers in an environment that celebrates innovation and thinking. In Chapter 8 we close the text with how to take these ideas and approaches forward. We believe the best ideas for teaching and learning are those that have the potential to grow; you will imbue your classroom activities with ideas from your own mental models of problem solving and investigating.

References

Department for Education. (2013). *The national curriculum for England and Wales.* London, UK: DfE.

Hargreaves, A. (2003). *Teaching in the knowledge society.* Maidenhead, UK: McGraw-Hill Education.

Understanding thinking
Mental models and why they are relevant to classrooms

Thinking differently

It was when I started teaching in the early 1980s that I comprehended the significance of the different ways people think. Teaching small children to read, write and calculate challenged my hitherto unexamined ways of thinking, and I started to reflect more deeply about differences in thinking. It may be that I was particularly naïve or that the easy-going nature of my family and friends provided a cocoon that protected me from having to defend my decisions or ways of thinking. Even three years of 'teacher training' did not challenge me to interrogate my comfortable and seemingly successful ways of thinking. The act of teaching with the requisite skill of communicating clearly new ideas and ways of learning to a large group of six-year-olds removed any assumptions I had about the homogeneity of thought! It was a revelation and catapulted me on a pathway of learning that continues today.

Twenty years later I undertook Master's studies that led me into the realms of cognitive theory and particularly Mental Model Theory. One of the ways that I use to explain the idea of mental models is by using analogy and metaphor. The difference between Mental Model Theory and other theories that use schemes or scripts to explain how information is processed is to equate it to walking into a dark room for the first time. When I ask others what they would do first they reply that they would brush their free hand (not the one holding the doorknob) against the wall inside the doorway to feel for the light switch. When asked why they would act in such a way they respond that they had learned this action from experience; entering a dark room and turning on the light switch was enacting a scheme that Piaget (1970) suggested is learned through assimilation and/or accommodation so as to be able to act in the world. Actions such as this 'light-switch schema' are stored in our long-term memory and enable us to act unconsciously and usually successfully in day-to-day life. But what happens when you can't find a light switch? People ponder this query for a while, because it seems such a redundant question. They usually respond that, although the room is strange to them, they understand that because it is a functional room within the building and is used both day and night, there should be a light source in it somewhere. They explain they would walk beside the wall, brushing their hand against it so as to reach a switch or a piece of furniture upon which a lamp could be sitting so they can switch it on. Some suggest waving their hands in the air to trigger a sensor light. These actions, I suggest, are the result of their running mental models; they are retrieving and using cognitive structures that are different to schemes because mental models allow them to act in *novel* situations using a *variety* of memories and knowledge to find a solution rather than employing one route to solve the problem.

What the study of mental models also highlights is an understanding of the mismatches of thought that often occur between people. Why is it that we think differently? What can account for lack of understanding? Breakdown in or lack of communication can be as much about mismatching mental models as it can be about the stubborn defence of oppositional ideas or the lack of clarity about new knowledge. The theory of mental models provides a rich and useful explanation, particularly for teachers, about how individuals use their memory and make connections with often innovative strategies to find solutions to vexing problems. Barker, van Schaik and Hudson (1998, p. 104) explained their usefulness succinctly by stating that they "form the basis of all human behaviour". If this is so, then an exploration of mental models can be illuminative, enabling teachers to better understand the cognitive, physical and social behaviour of their students. We'll start this exploration by looking at what mental models are. But finding a categorical definition for mental models is quite challenging in itself, and one of the difficulties arises due to the use of the term 'model'.

Understanding how we think

Most individuals believe they understand (they have a mental model for!) what constitutes a model; a model is a representation of some object or process. In essence we can create *a model* of a phenomenon or we can *model* it. However, the noun/verb nature of the word is a paradox because it is simultaneously useful and confusing. As a product, a mental model is "created by individuals who have used their cognitive functions in the broadest possible way to create a representation or structure of the phenomenon or solution to a problem" (Edwards-Leis, 2013a, p. 17). But a mental model can 'contain' many components including concepts, processes, and propositional knowledge as well as beliefs, emotions and judgments. As a process, the mental models are run in the act of mental modelling to solve a problem or find a solution to a conundrum, a puzzle or a missing light switch! The result of running one or many connected mental models will be the creation or refinement of more useful mental models that the individual will then store for later use because the solution has been

Understanding thinking

evaluated as functional. It is useful now to visit earlier studies to understand how mental models are positioned in cognitive science.

Taxonomies, such as Bloom's (1956) on higher-order thinking, can be illuminative. Kyllonnen and Shute (1989) also created a useful one of knowledge types that demonstrated the difference between mental models and other cognitive structures such as schemata. Propositions were their baseline structures composed of simple declarative or propositional knowledge that may include abstract symbols and definitions of single items (Johnson-Laird, 1983). Examples of these in the Primary mathematics classroom would be the recognition of the numeric symbols 1, 2, 3 to represent the natural numbers. Propositional *if-then* representations follow from this baseline of knowledge types and include such processes as '*if* adding one *then* put one more block in the pile'. Jonassen (1995), who has undertaken intensive research in problem solving, suggests that propositions are a prerequisite for the acquisition of schemes.

Kyllonnen and Shute (1989) agreed, suggesting that schemata are formed by developing a network of related propositional representations or knowledge which have been formed due to previous experiences and understanding. They proposed that individuals draw on the schemata they have stored in long-term memory to determine how the propositional representations relate to phenomena in the environment that may be involved in the current investigation. My co-author tells an enjoyable story about her daughter as a way of illustrating how early individuals network their experiences. She had agreed with her husband not to give their children too many sugary snacks so limited their biscuit consumption to plain digestive biscuits. Debbie's chocolate addiction was served by a hidden supply of chocolate-coated digestives, several of which were presented to the children as little rewards on occasion, always when her partner was not at home. Some time after the secretive chocolate treats had begun, her partner gave their younger child, Helen, aged 18 months, a plain digestive and was surprised at her reaction of constantly flipping the biscuit over in her hands. Debbie saw firsthand Helen's display of the network of stored experiences as she tried to find the chocolate which she had learned was associated with the digestive biscuit. Helen clearly understood and enjoyed the chocolate digestives as much as Debbie, and a bemused husband had uncovered the chocolate stash!

The formation of such individual networks is also of great interest to teachers because how students store and subsequently retrieve information influences the planning they do for effective instruction. Teachers want children not only to learn new things but also to remember them, and that is why rhyme, music and literature (rather than chocolate) are used so much by teachers working with early-years students to learn to count and recognize natural numbers. The context of the experience or what Askew (2012) recommended as the connectionist approach is what enables the student to make sense of the experience by linking it to something they understand. Such rich, contextualized and connected experiences can offer some success in applying

7

Understanding thinking

appropriate strategies and subsequently guide or encourage them to effectively store the experiences because of those related, meaningful understandings.

Creating networks of ideas

Kyllonnen and Shute (1989) suggested that individuals create networks because they are important, and in the case of the 'light-switch schema' the actions are constantly run and include everyday experiences and objects. In order to create a network of these representations the individual must categorize and compartmentalize the knowledge in ways that make sense to them. This meaningful sorting implies that understanding how to group objects is a fundamental prerequisite for being able to store information in useful ways. Piaget's (1970) discussion of schema through such descriptors as 'all four-legged animals are dogs' makes sense when we look at children's early attempts at grouping objects into useful categories. Such grouping and sorting mental models are particularly useful for children in Year One, in which the English and Welsh curriculum (DfE, 2013), not too dissimilar to curriculum documents in other Western countries, requires children to group and share quantities in development of multiplication and division concepts. It is fundamental to effective planning in mathematics classrooms, then, that all information is delivered and presented in ways that allow children to group or categorize the information being presented so that the compartmentalization process can facilitate the storage of the knowledge.

Schemas are aggregations of the simple sub-schemas often referred to as scripts. In the 'light switch schema' a sub-schema or script would be to *turn the handle of the door* in order to gain access to the room. Another would be the act of *moving the light switch to an opposite position* to either create or remove light. In the Primary mathematics classroom a sub-schema may be as simple as *collecting a plastic tape measure* (1.5m) from the resource shelf because the student has been asked to measure specific parts of their environment, such as around parts of their body, for a measurement activity. Just as individuals learn how to turn a knob to open a door, students in classrooms use previous experiences such as using a tape measure to measure something long and non-rigid to inform them of the required action to collect a known object to complete a required task that has some similarity. Linking sub-schema creates useful networks.

Schemas are useful and allow us to act in circumstances similar to the original arena of occurrence. However, just as when we enter a darkened room and the light switch cannot be easily found by running a sub-schema, we are often faced with situations for which an existing schema or sub-schema is of little use by itself because of its inability to solve the problem at hand. Merrill and Gilbert (2008) compared schema to mental models when they investigated the comparative effectiveness of problem-centred learning to learner-centred learning and concluded that while schema tend towards stability because of their reliability through replication, mental models are often transient. They found that mental models are cognitive structures "related together in a meaningful way in a holistic representation of the parts, relationships, conditions, actions, and consequences of a complete problem or task" (Merrill & Gilbert, 2008, p. 201). An individual will modify the retrieved mental models as they work through a problem, and during this process the mental models used will be modified or expanded to account for the unprecedented experience. Learning occurs as the transient mental models evolve into new and more useful structures that the individual will subsequently store in long-term memory for future use.

But teachers would be aware of the difficulties students may have in solving challenging tasks when they are required to instantiate new procedural and propositional knowledge. Sometimes students are stalled in the problem-solving process because they are trying to hold too much in their heads at one time. This stalled learning is a type of cognitive blister (Edwards-Leis, 2013b) in which the constant reworking of ineffective strategies results in the student not making progress and tiring of repeated attempts to find solutions. The use of various strategies including making annotations, drawing diagrams or using manipulatives during mathematical inquiry can be useful. But what does Mental Model Theory offer in way of explanation of the processes that are occurring, and what can be done to facilitate better use of working memory so students can learn to investigate more effectively?

Memory and making best use of space

Working memory is an interesting concept to explain to students both young and old. I often use an analogy of working memory and the school desk. If a student is using their work space efficiently they need to leave as much room as they can for the actual working out, whether it be constructing a model with multilink cubes or drawing a diagram on A4 paper. If they have other materials on the desk that are of use in creating their response to a task such as books, pencils, rulers or paints, then they need to place them thoughtfully so as to leave the room required for presentation of a solution. I remind student teachers of what happens when they are writing an assignment: they will often place texts in a pile on their desk so as to avoid them dropping onto the floor as they delve into different ones in search of information. More often than not, though, books are scattered across any available space! However, the use of sticky notes enables the individual to mark useful places in texts so that retrieval of appropriate information is stored externally to the individual yet in a way that is idiosyncratically understood. The annotating of information this way means that we can sort information externally so that it is readily accessible in similar ways that we can store information internally in our long-term memory for retrieval for future activity.

Miller's (1956) seminal work on the effective use of working memory established its limitations of seven plus or minus two pieces of discrete information that can be reliably managed at any one time. Baddeley's (2010) later work confirmed this limitation of memory storage span, and interesting results also came from Gathercole, Alloway, Willis and Adams (2006). They worked in education with children at risk and found that tasks that required complex processing particularly constrained the acquisition of mathematical skills. Baddeley (2010) affirmed the relationship between long-term memory and working memory due to the existence of neuroimaging studies of working memory activities showing links through the activation of both relative areas of the brain. Gathercole et al. (2006, p. 280) suggested that "working memory acts as a bottleneck for learning in classroom activities" and made suggestions about how teachers can assist children to move past such constraints to improve their learning potential. Johnson-Laird (2008) suggests that we can determine working memory by measuring how many digits we can hold in our mind at one time. While most adults replicate Miller's (1956) findings of around seven, which is the average length of some phone numbers (pre-mobile days though), Johnson-Laird (2008) suggests children at age three can cope with only three digits, four-year-olds with four digits, and finally by seven children should be working comfortably with seven digits. This improvement, he suggests, is due to maturing brains and the development of knowledge. Working memory limitation, therefore, is a serious concern when preparing lessons, and teachers' understanding of mental models can help them prepare children better for efficient and effective problem solving.

Keeping working space efficient often means chunking information so as to bring together related information in useful segments, thereby relieving the stress of trying to hold too much information in the head at one time. Henderson and Tallman (2006) established during their research with librarians and Primary students that mental models constrain working memory overload because of how they bring what Merrill and Gilbert (2008) later termed propositional representations *and* schemas together to predict outcomes. Merrill and Gilbert's (2008) work on problem-centred learning established that the more complex the problem the more likely it is to limit working memory because working memory, regardless of age, cannot always hold, at one time, all the skills and knowledge required to find a solution. Earlier, Wild (1996, p. 10) also described the usefulness of mental models, suggesting that they are representations that provide a "mediating intervention between perception and action" which enables an individual to interpret what is required in an inquiry, recall the knowledge, materials and processes required to enact a solution and communicate the results to others. The subsequent impact of Mental Model Theory on communication has been substantial and relevant to many fields including business (Senge, 1996) and language comprehension and semantic reasoning (Johnson-Laird, 1983) because it addresses working memory problems and how we manage the process of thinking and problem solving. The next chapter on the functions of mental models and the Mental Model

Understanding thinking

Mode will describe how mental models can be controlled to enact problem-solving strategies and processes more effectively.

How mental models enable collaborative work

Teachers work to develop students' abilities to communicate what they know in a variety of ways. The expression of knowledge in writing, oral discourse or dramatic genres such as visual arts or design is at the forefront of teachers' planning for classroom interactions. Early research by Johnson-Laird (1983) continues to be relevant to teachers in this area because it focuses on mental models and language comprehension. It is useful to consider language comprehension not simplistically as a spoken linguistic construct but more wholly as a means of communicating knowledge. Johnson-Laird's work used mental models as the mechanism by which reasoning could be understood by focusing more on semantic content than the syntactic, as would be evident in the more traditional symbolic logic theories.

Students use symbolic representation, particularly in mathematics, where they decode information on whiteboards, smart boards and textbooks or in their environment. The decoding that students in Year One and Two do when interpreting and subsequently manipulating the processes and quantities required to work through simple addition or subtraction algorithms is complex. Johnson-Laird and Byrne (1991 confirmed that when students decode such symbols as '+' or '−' the action becomes an internal one in which new understandings are created through inference and then translated into external actions through reasoning, which is one of three aims of the new mathematics curriculum in England and Wales (DfE, 2013) and not dissimilar to curriculum requirements in mathematics in other Western jurisdictions. The reasoning process results in the construction of more functional mental models that represent the interaction and incorporate the relevant concepts of the phenomenon being worked on, the methods tested and enacted to find a solution, the solution itself and any relevant sensory or affective input encountered while undertaking the investigation. This rich content means that mental models are much more complex than the relatively compact schemes that Piaget (1970) suggested were so useful to construct meaning. Mental models are not only laden with abundant information but also imbued with the essence of the individual and how they make sense of their world.

Social constructivist theory (Vygotsky, 1978) made propositions about how an individual conceptualizes and creates cognitive representations, such as mental models, from internalizing experiences with others. Individuals distribute or share what they know with others when they use any means to communicate. Norman (1983, p. 77) looked at "knowledge in the world" and "knowledge in the head", proposing that often some knowledge is left out of mental models because the model contains links or procedures that will enable sought-after information to be found when required. This processing is a similar to 'just-in-time' manufacturing or production, in which the next step in the production process is enacted only when needed thereby eliminating a great deal of waste from the manufacturing process. Rather than storing information, or inventories, in case it is needed, the producer (in this case the student) retrieves information either from their memory or from the environment when they have judged or diagnosed the need for it to solve a problem. Such processing approaches also reduce space taken up in working memory with extraneous, often unnecessary items, thereby making the problem-solving process more efficient.

O'Malley and Draper (1992) addressed the distinction between types of knowledge and how information can be stored and accessed in mental models in a study of the use of computer menus. They concluded that enough information is often stored in mental models to locate other information when required but not the actual information itself. For example, an individual may know that they can add page numbers to a document being created by a word processor but not necessarily know the menu item to select to do so. The process to add the page number is understood, but the precise menu item to do so is not. While the individual may resort to using the 'help' function to eventually find what they are looking for, they are enacting the semantic reasoning processes to find the necessary menu choice, a reasoning process that Johnson-Laird (1983) suggested was a particular feature of mental models. This self-selection of useable information enables mental models to be more streamlined, and while it may appear that mental models are more fragmented because they don't need to be complete to be useful, it demonstrates how they rely on the network of related understandings to trigger the actions required to complete the task.

Working with others

When students work collaboratively to investigate mathematically, they must share dialogue that involves the manipulation of a shared mental model (Henderson & Tallman, 2006; Senge, 1992). Anderson, Howe and Tolmie (1996) suggest that the shared mental model that evolves from the contribution of several individual mental models will be superior, and this phenomenon can be quite evident when listening to groups of students who are conducting an investigation. The ideas they are generating almost sit like a creative soup between the members of the group as they dip in, add and blend their contributions. Some ideas might be quite elaborate and unworkable, but the creative activity of posing ideas can be exciting and contribute to later thoughts and imaginings. The shared mental model is transitory (Anderson et al., 1996) and external while it is being created, becoming internal when each individual moves away from the collaboration and stores it, imbuing it with idiosyncratic beliefs, understandings and interpretations. To test this I would suggest giving a group of three students a task to complete collaboratively. Once complete ask each student to explain verbally using diagrams or concept maps what they worked on. Each explanation will be quite different in several ways because it has been coloured by the individual perceptions and preferences of each student.

There are, of course, implications for group formation when considering students working collaboratively to investigate mathematically. The quality of the dialogue that occurs within the group will be dependent on the richness of the mental models (Barker et al., 1998) that the students bring to the collaboration. Polanyi's (1966, p. 4) explanation of tacit knowing that describes how individuals "know more than we can tell" indicates that knowledge can be deeply personalized and difficult to articulate. He explained how students approach new knowledge often with an acceptance of a teacher's authority or their view of knowledge and will then start to create meaning for themselves. This action is also relevant when students work with others to complete a collaborative task because the authority of the group, or perhaps the one with the loudest voice within it, may influence the interpretation of what understandings are required to complete it and therefore what mental models are retrieved and run during and subsequently stored after the event. Therefore, providing students with a variety of individuals to work with will enable them to gain a deeper understanding of how they interact with others and judge their ideas. Some group work will be more rewarding than others, and this may be due to the topic or the collaborators. Limiting collaborative experiences because students may feel uncomfortable is not sufficient reason to abandon group investigations. Comfort zones should be challenged so as to provide the disequilibrium (Piaget, 1970) or perturbation (Ritchie, Tobin & Hook, 1997) required for learning to occur. Learning how to appreciate the ideas of others and work with them to investigate new ideas is challenging but offers significant opportunities for children to learn more about their own mental models and why they may be different to others in the class.

Differentiation in the classroom: novice and expert mental models in learning

Setting by ability is an unfortunate reality in many schools in England as well as other Western countries and is often selected as an organizational strategy to reduce the spread of attainment to make life easier for the teacher. Alexander (2010) suggests that evidence shows that there are no consistent effects on attainment of streaming students in ability groups, or setting, and in fact there may be detrimental effects on social outcomes for the students. The latest mathematics curriculum document in England and Wales (DfE, 2013) suggests a mastery approach whereby children aren't set and the same lesson, in the main, is taught to all children. A consideration of

Mental Model Theory and its recognition of the idiosyncratic way that all individuals interact with the world would result in even fewer instances of streaming by ability. The use of the term 'set' is quite offensive indicating as it does the permanence of ability quite in opposition to the work of Dweck (2006) and her advocacy of growth over fixed mindsets. But an exploration of expert and novice mental models, while having a possible impact on how teachers may differentiate experiences for the students in their mathematics classrooms, does not presuppose an organizational structure on the environment and those who populate it. It opens for us a consideration of the different ways that individuals act if they have developed expertise in different areas of mathematics with implications for the kind of investigations that might best challenge students.

Students who are operating with novice mental models in a particular area of mathematics often lack the repertoire of cognitive representations that include conceptual, procedural and propositional knowledge necessary to respond to the inquiry with depth (Newton, 1996) in a timely way. An example might be a student who will understand that they need to share some money between several people (conceptual knowledge) but lack the procedural knowledge to do so. Their approaches to solving such a problem may deal with the 'surface' features and details in a linear fashion, which would result in the students doing repeated subtraction to reach a solution that would clearly take longer to enact than would the use of the division algorithm. It may not matter how they reach a solution as long as they work towards one. However, having a better understanding of why they are selecting particular strategies can be informative for teachers. Encouraging the students themselves to understand the way they solve problems and enact mathematical strategies is also liberating, because it begins to focus on the externalization of the thinking process; it exteriorizes the mental modelling that is occurring so errors in thinking and processing can be exposed for remediation.

Experts not only have the required conceptual, procedural and propositional knowledge to act decisively, but such knowledge is hierarchically stored with broader strategies above the narrower ones below, which enables them to function more successfully and strategically (Newton, 1996). Not only do they have the *depth* of knowledge well stored because it has been logically sorted, but they can make appropriate *selection* of this knowledge in new situations (Sloboda, 1996). It is this selection and deployment of appropriate knowledge (Newton, 1996; Sloboda, 1996) in novel investigations that distinguishes the expert from the novice. I recall a 10-year-old student from a project on robotics. She was teaching another student to use the equipment and programme as part of a teach-back data collection episode (Edwards-Leis, 2013c). When the robot continued to go in the opposite direction to the one she had programmed even after repeating the steps in her 'problem-solving' strategy, the student denied it had responded incorrectly and told her 'pupil' to "leave it there and see the next thing" (Edwards-Leis, 2013c, p. 228). Denial was her only option because

Understanding thinking

she did not have the mental models available to enact any other strategy to correct the error.

Some interesting research was conducted by Leviton in 2003 in which the communication of risk information in a medical context was studied. Leviton (2003, p. 529) found that the expert's mental model was "highly elaborated" while that of the novice (layperson) was "sketchy and . . . quickly exhausted". The novice's mental model also contained "key mistaken beliefs" (Leviton, 2003, p. 529), which while of extreme concern in a medical situation may be less so in a Primary mathematics classroom in the short term. Nevertheless, the inaccuracies of a student's mental model need to be addressed and remedied, and in order to do this they first need to be recognized. If children are working with others who are operating with robust and useful mental models, for example understanding how to share by using the division algorithm rather than repeated subtraction, they are more likely to run and manipulate their mental model for this when working closely alongside such an expert rather than in a group of similarly engaged students. Over time, experts develop functional mental models in particular areas due to the retrieval of several mental models that are run in parallel and interlinked (Henderson & Tallman, 2006), making them more secure and useful for finding solutions. A novice may select limited mental models from a narrower field rather than the broader strategies used by experts (Newton, 1996). The implications for mathematics in the classroom are unambiguous; children need many opportunities to test their knowledge and ideas with others in order to develop the repertoire of robust mental models necessary to be successful problem solvers.

Response times are also of interest to teachers who are conducting investigations in mathematics, because providing sufficient time for students to reach a satisfying conclusion is necessary for them to create the mental models necessary for expert use. What is of interest is that a study by Britton and Tesser (1982) discovered that knowledgeable students or experts often had significantly longer investigation time due to their having less processing capacity of their working memory because of the retrieval of a multitude of mental models at one time. Novices, on the other hand, had greater capacity in their working memory because they were retrieving fewer mental models to address the investigation. This paradox can be evident in the mathematics classroom when students have completed a seemingly complex investigation very quickly. In fact, when the teacher reviews their work they have been found to skim over the complex aspects of the investigation and arrived at an inaccurate or incomplete answer. Williamson (1999, p. 21) found that novices have mental models that are "fragmented, incomplete, and inaccurate" due mostly to the limited experience they have in using them in novel situations that provide sufficient time and support to complete tasks successfully. So providing repeated tasks that are time rich in a space that enables prolonged thinking is more likely to promote robust, rich and useful mental models that can be called upon when required to enable solutions to problems to be found.

15

Understanding thinking

Where next?

This chapter has introduced you to the idea of mental models. It has hopefully encouraged you to think more deeply about how you, as a teacher of mathematics, plan for, support and evaluate the problem-solving activities in your classroom. As the text progresses, you will be encouraged to think more specifically about certain aspects of your pedagogical practice. The next chapter introduces the functions of mental models and the Mental Model Mode. This construct should provide a clearer picture of how problem solving in the Primary mathematics classroom can be supported more confidently because of a deeper understanding of what children will be thinking at different stages of the problem-solving process.

References

Alexander, R. (2010). *Children, their world, their education: Final report and recommendations of the Cambridge primary review.* Oxon, UK: Routledge.

Anderson, T., Howe, C., & Tolmie, A. (1996). Interaction and mental models of physics phenomena: Evidence from dialogues between learners. In J. Oakhill & A. Garnham (Eds.), *Mental models in cognitive science* (pp. 247–273). East Sussex, UK: Psychology Press.

Askew, M. (2012). *Transforming primary mathematics.* Oxon, UK: Routledge.

Baddeley, A. (2010). Working memory. *Current Biology, 20*(4), 136–140.

Barker, P., van Schaik, P., & Hudson, S. (1998). Mental models and lifelong learning. *Innovations in Education and Training International, 35*(4), 310–319.

Bloom, B. S. (Ed.). (1956). *Taxonomy of educational objectives, the classification of educational goals – handbook I: Cognitive domain.* New York, NY: McKay.

Britton, B. K., & Tesser, A. (1982). Effects of prior knowledge on use of cognitive capacity in three complex cognitive tasks. *Journal of Verbal Learning and Verbal Behaviour, 21*, 421–436.

Department for Education (2013). *The national curriculum for England and Wales.* London, UK: DfE.

Dweck, C. S. (2006). *Mindset: The new psychology of success.* New York, NY: Random House.

Edwards-Leis, C. E. (2013a). Where are they going wrong? Finding solutions to problems using the Mental Model Mode. In J. West-Burnham, M. James, & J. Renowden (Eds.), *Rethinking the curriculum: Embedding moral and spiritual growth in teaching and learning* (pp. 96–115). Bath, UK: Brown Dog Books.

16

Edwards-Leis, C. E. (2013b). Knowing where the shoe pinches: Using the Mental Model Mode to understand how primary pupils can design intelligently. In *Technology education for the future: A play on sustainability, PATT27 Conference* (pp. 141–148). Christchurch, NZ: University of Waikato.

Edwards-Leis, C. E. (2013c). *Understanding learning through Mental Model Theory.* Saarbrücken, Germany: LAP Lambert Academic Publishing.

Gathercole, S. E., Alloway, T. P., Willis, C., & Adams, A. (2006). Working memory children with reading disabilities. *Journal of Experimental Child Psychology, 93,* 265–281.

Henderson, L., & Tallman, J. (2006). *Stimulated recall and mental models.* Lanham, MD: Scarecrow Press, Inc.

Johnson-Laird, P. N. (1983). *Mental models: Towards a cognitive science of language, inference, and consciousness.* Cambridge, MA: Harvard University Press.

Johnson-Laird, P. N. (2008). *How we reason.* Oxford, UK: Oxford University Press.

Johnson-Laird, P. N., & Byrne, R. M. J. (1991). *Deduction.* Hillsdale, NJ: Lawrence Erlbaum.

Jonassen, D. H. (1995). *Operationalizing mental models: Strategies for assessing mental models to support meaningful learning and design – supportive learning environments.* Pennsylvania State University. Retrieved November 26, 2003, from www.ittheory.com/jonassen2.htm

Kyllonen, P. C., & Shute, V. J. (1989). A taxonomy of learning skills. In P. L. Ackerman, R. J. Sternberg, & R. Glaser (Eds.), *Learning and individual differences: Advances in theory and research* (pp. 117–163). New York, NY: W. H. Freeman and Company.

Leviton, L. C. (2003). Evaluation use: Advances, challenges and applications. *American Journal of Evaluation, 24,* 525–535.

Merrill, D. M., & Gilbert, C. B. (2008). Effective peer interaction in a problem-centred instructional strategy. *Distant Education, 29*(2), 109–207.

Miller, G. (1956). The magical number seven, plus or minus two: Some limits on our capacity for processing information. *Psychological Review, 63,* 81–97.

Newton, D. (1996). Causal situations in science: A model for supporting understanding. In R. Saljo (Ed.), *Learning and instruction* (Vol. 6(3), pp. 201–217). Great Britain: Elsevier Science Ltd.

Norman, D. A. (1983). Some observations on mental models. In D. Gentner & A. L. Stevens (Eds.), *Mental models* (pp. 7–14). Hillsdale, NJ: Lawrence Erlbaum.

O'Malley, C., & Draper, S. (1992). Representation and interaction: Are mental models all in the mind? In Y. Rogers, A. Rutherford, & P. Bibby (Eds.), *Models in the mind: Theory, perspective and application* (pp. 73–92). London, UK: Academic Press.

Piaget, J. (1970). *The science of education and the psychology of the child.* New York, NY: Orion Press.

Polanyi, M. (1966). *The tacit dimension.* London, UK: University of Chicago Press.

Ritchie, S. M., Tobin, K., & Hook, K. S. (1997). Teaching referents and the warrants used to test the viability of students' mental models: Is there a link? *Journal of Research in Science Training, 34*(3), 223–238.

Senge, P. M. (1992). Mental models. *Planning Review, 20*(2), 4–44.

Senge, P. M. (1996). *The fifth discipline: The art and practice of the learning organization.* London, UK: Random House.

Sloboda, J. (1996). The acquisition of musical performance expertise: Deconstructing the "talent" account of individual differences in musical expressivity. In K. Ericsson (Ed.), *The road to excellence: The acquisition of expert performance in the arts and sciences, sports and games* (pp. 107–126). Mahwah, NJ: Lawrence Erlbaum.

Vygotsky, L. S. (1978). *Mind in society.* Cambridge, MA: Harvard University Press.

Wild, M. (1996). Mental models and computer modeling. *Journal of Computer Assisted Learning, 12,* 10–21.

Williamson, J. W. (1999). *Mental models of teaching: Case study of selected pre-service teachers enrolled in an introductory educational technology course* (Doctoral dissertation). The University of Georgia, Athens, GA.

2 The functions of thinking

Introduction

Chapter 1 introduced you to the significance of mental models. This chapter explains how a richer understanding of how the mental model functions support reasoning helps you to create challenging activities that promote mathematical reasoning for the pupils in your class. Establishing and implementing stimulating activities for pupils makes for very exciting pedagogical practice because of the uncertainty of some outcomes and the abundant opportunities to develop new knowledge that are possible. One of the aims of the national curriculum of England and Wales (DfE, 2013), which is also evident in Primary mathematic curricula around the world, is to provide opportunities for children to reason mathematically. Reasoning means to follow some type of logical pathway of thinking or, as Johnson-Laird (2008, p. 3) says, contains "a set of processes that construct and evaluate implications among sets of propositions". Reasoning is procedural, and while suggesting that the thinking involved follows a 'pathway', it is clear that it can get a bit messy at times. If we consider Johnson-Laird's (2008) definition that includes the creation and evaluation of the effect of a range of possible solutions of an investigation, then we begin to appreciate the 'messiness' that is probable for mathematical reasoning activity because of the individual ways of constructing and evaluating understanding.

Embracing messiness in your mathematics lessons may seem a step too far for many teachers. If we interrogate what actually can happen in a messy mathematics activity it may help convince many of you that such intentional activities (Pring, 2010) have purpose and are able to sit comfortably within the controlling function of your mental models of teaching. An example I can give from my practice of teaching Year Four children in Australia will be illuminating and will reveal the extent to which the pupils' fears of the unknown and their desire for knowledge (Pring, 2010) contributed to an enjoyable activity that sat well within the requirements of the curriculum

The functions of thinking

The class I was to work with for several weeks was unfamiliar, so I had not established a relationship with the pupils. When the children were preparing for their first mathematics activity with me, they were surprised to have a plastic container, the size of a lunchbox, placed on their tables. Pupils sat in groups of four which were not formed by ability. Each box contained 30 or so different laundry or clothes pegs. The children were curious and found the situation a bit unusual until I told them that I wanted them to decide which was the *best* peg in their box (see Chapter 6: Rich tasks and big questions). After a bit of noise in which they expressed their disbelief and humour at being asked such a silly question, they settled down, and I started to see hands raised around the class.

They had many questions, which were answered with questions and prompts from me. The pupils soon realized that the nature and purpose of laundry or clothes pegs would contribute to how they would proceed to test each to determine the *best* peg. An example of such critical thinking was that if the peg needed to clip a wet towel to a clothesline and it was a windy day, then the peg needed to be able to hold a considerable weight. From this knowledge and understanding, the pupils asked how they might test each peg to see how much it could hold before it broke or released the item it was holding. One child remembered his grandfather using a spring scale to weigh their travel bags, so we sourced some of these for the children to design and conduct their tests. The activity continued, with increasingly complex tests, over the next few weeks, during which most of the mathematics the children were doing was embedded in their efforts to design, test, calculate and record the results of their investigations. They were using the different operations including fractions, measurement such as time and weight, as well as statistics for recording. What started life as a *big question* became a very refined and orderly investigation for specific attributes requiring cooperation and collaboration between pupils.

There were six groups in the class, and their results at the end were quite similar but not the same, and this difference was also the stimulus for additional discourse in which we, as a group of investigators, evaluated the validity of the testing undertaken and the quality of the results found. Mathematics became real because it involved a critique of a real-life issue, and even if such issues are often messy our way of dealing with them can be organized, which was also a valuable lesson. I think most parents were quite surprised when their children developed what seemed like an unhealthy interest in the clothes pegs. More to the point, some were delighted that their children would talk enthusiastically about what they were doing in mathematics each day. My decision to do the activity and subsequent observations of it in progress aligned with those of Jonassen (2011), who is a strong proponent of context. He suggests that "instruction should establish and elaborate a context, because information acquired in a real-world context is better retained, the learning that results is more generative, higher order, and more meaningful" (Jonassen, 2011, p. 210). The activity was certainly memorable for me and while challenging at times due to its

The functions of thinking

seemingly chaotic nature, had a life of its own that brought children together purposefully and productively.

Finding time for investigations

Creating opportunities for open-ended explorations in Primary mathematics is fundamental for the provision of the mental space and intellectually stimulating environment for children necessary to make new understandings. The constraints of a classroom are not only the physical boundaries around it but also the impact of other organizational school activities that influence the length of time that may be allowed for pupils to follow an investigation. Given that mathematical reasoning activities can be quite open ended and that children have different mental models, interests and levels of confidence, the provision of adequate time to provide the space for reasoning can be quite complex to organize and therefore a challenge in itself for most Primary teachers.

Extended time for thinking is seldom available in a busy, modern classroom in which the pressure of curriculum requirements means that pupils need to move from one subject or activity to another so as to 'get through' the required material. Yet time is the very component of reasoning that is most necessary to enable children to develop the skills and attitudes necessary to follow a line of inquiry. The latest curriculum document for England and Wales (DfE, 2013, p. 3) acknowledges this by suggesting "decisions about when to progress should always be based on the security of pupils' understanding and their readiness to progress to the next stage". The document also gives some guidance on the type of questions teachers will ask when designing mathematical activities: What if some pupils finish within the time allowed during the initial time of inquiry and others do not? What are the implications for time management and organization of learning space and provision of activities for learning if different groups of pupils are at different places in the inquiry? While no one text can provide all of the answers, the aims of the curriculum suggest that pupils who gain understanding quickly should be offered "rich and sophisticated problems before any acceleration through new content" (DfE, 2013, p. 3). These problems do not have to take onerous planning by teachers; they can emerge from the context of children's lives.

Planning for different activities in the classroom including such inquiries can be messy. However, embracing 'messy' may be the most useful way forward if teachers and their pupils are to develop the attitudes to risk taking and individuality that should permeate the Primary mathematics classroom. Perhaps welcoming the butterfly effect would also enable teachers and their pupils to better understand the consequences that Edward Lorenz suggested come from small changes in non-linear systems such as a Primary classroom. Small changes in how we accommodate the needs of children of all abilities such as providing rich, open-ended work can have significant and unforeseen effects. One foreseeable outcome will be that pupils will develop more robust and *effective* mental models of problem solving through developing the mastery that the DfE (2013) see as necessary when learning mathematics.

What we can also predict is the necessity of teachers and their pupils having a clear understanding of how mental models enable them to perform in mathematical investigations. The specific study of the functions of mental models appears in various projects including Henderson and Tallman (2006), who worked with teacher librarians and their pupils as they used the Internet to search for information. A study I conducted with Primary pupils undertaking problem solving in robotics established more clarity around several functions that enabled them to make progress in investigations (see Edwards-Leis, 2013a). This chapter will now describe the various functions of mental models and how they aid the progress of pupils through inquiries. It explains how when the functions work together they frame the Mental Model Mode, a construct designed to demonstrate how information can be worked on to create plausible solutions to inquiries. The chapter will conclude with a review of the Mode Typology that provides a scaffold to support teachers and their pupils as they work through investigations, highlighting the mental model functions and how they enhance performance.

The functions of thinking and how to prompt specific action in the classroom

What is of most interest to teachers in the Primary classroom is that mental models have multiple functions; they enable individuals to undertake a variety of reasoning tasks. Norman (1983) characterized mental models as idiosyncratic, and this description is useful to remind us that pupils will bring quite different ways of thinking to the mathematical activities designed by their teachers. Teachers may present what they believe are complete and unambiguous instructions, but the way that this information is processed, understood and acted on can vary significantly from pupil to pupil due to their individual views and experiences of the world. What teachers can take heart from is the work of Norman (1983) and Jonassen (2011), who not only recommended that pupils should construct their own mental models of the problem at hand but affirmed the functionality of mental models regardless of this uniqueness.

The affirmation that mental models are functional does not mean that they will all operate correctly or accurately on every occasion: an individual will not store a mental model, retaining the conceptual, procedural and propositional knowledge embedded in it, unless it serves some purpose for them to do so, and sometimes an incorrect mental model is stored because the individual believes it to be true and purposeful. An example of an incorrect mental model being stored was seen when Debbie was working with an undergraduate student teacher who was calculating the possible combinations of a seating arrangements for three people by adding 3 + 2 + 1 rather than calculating it correctly as factorial 3 or 3 × 2 × 1. This incorrect process was based on her limited previous experience and had always been accurate because of the numbers she had been exploring. She had retained an inaccurate mental model of calculating all possible combinations because she had seemed only to have worked with this unique combination for which both methods resulted in the correct answer which was 6. Therefore, providing many opportunities to test, evaluate and reconfigure or refine incorrect mental models is a necessary part of the learning process. This fundamental understanding has an important implication for teachers: if they want pupils to develop and retain mental models for all of the areas of mathematics relevant to age, then they need to ensure that the pupils see some value or purpose in doing so. Askew's (2012) emphasis on connectionism is paramount in ensuring children are exposed to meaningful learning episodes that enable them to act purposefully to construct rich, robust and *relevant* mental models of mathematics.

Functions of mental models

Mental models reflect an individual's interactions with the world including connections with the people with whom they come in contact, the environments they exist within, the situations they find themselves engaged in, the tasks they do, procedures they follow, concepts they encounter and any other phenomena that contribute to their reality. The mental models held by individuals arise from their constant, often complex experiences with the world and from the reactions to and results of their efforts to interact with, experience and understand that world. Therefore, mental models have complex performance demands because they enable individuals to manage their world, hopefully with success but sometimes with less triumph than they may have hoped. The more challenging interactions we have, the more likely we are to learn. The following sections outline the functions of mental models that are relevant to all of us but of particular interest to teachers who are providing learning experiences for pupils in the Primary classroom.

Explaining the world

One of the more unambiguous functions of mental models is the explanation function. Henderson and Tallman (2006, p. 25) described this function as the means to "facilitate cognitive and physical interactions with the environment, with others, and with artefacts". Johnson-Laird (1983, p. 2) outlined his interpretation of this function by suggesting:

> understanding certainly depends on knowledge and belief. If you know what causes a phenomenon, what results from it, how to influence, control, initiate,

The functions of thinking

or prevent it, how *it relates to other* states of affairs or how it resembles them, how to predict its onset and course, what its internal or underlying structure is, then to some extent you understand it.

He discussed individuals having a "working model" of the phenomena in their minds: understanding means a resultant representation that "serves as an entity" for it (Johnson-Laird, 1983, p. 3).

But explaining can be quite difficult, particularly for young children who are still developing their mathematical vocabulary and their understanding of cause and effect. Johnson-Laird (2008, p. 348) discussed many experiments that confirmed that the participants preferred "explanations that go beyond the minimal" when asked to come up with the most probable explanation for a variety of scenarios. In other words, people tend to evaluate cause and effect (rather than cause or effect singly) as the most probable explanation for an event. An example in a Primary classroom of this phenomenon would be to determine how many pieces of pizza each person would have if two pizzas were shared between four people.

1   A careful person had sliced each pizza into six equal pieces. (Cause only)

2   There were 12 pieces of pizza placed on the serving platter. (Effect only)

3   A careful person had sliced each pizza into six equal pieces, and there were 12 pieces placed on the serving platter. (Cause and effect)

The result is that 12 pieces were shared between four people giving each person 3 pieces. The result is the same for each of the explanations, but the *ways of explaining* are different. Therefore, modelling such processes of explaining is fundamental to pupils developing competence and confidence to explain new understandings and to accommodate new beliefs through the inclusion of small changes in the way that we explain what we know. A clear understanding of what is expected of pupils when they explain also prepares them well for other functions such as predicting what might happen if a particular action is taken.

Predicting what might happen

Another executive function of mental models that Johnson-Laird (1983) observed being used by research participants in language acquisition was predicting. Edwards-Leis (2013a) confirmed that pupils who were operating in a problem space with robotics also used prediction to anticipate the likelihood of success in their programming and construction of robots. Prediction is one of the functions that differentiate mental models from other cognitive structures such as schema because it enables the

The functions of thinking

individual to operate in a novel situation for which a schema would be ineffective. Jonassen (2011, p. 268) stated that "reasoning from a condition or set of conditions or states of an event to the possible effect(s) that may result from those states is called prediction". Predictions define the relationship that exists between cause and effect as shown earlier and are useful for enabling pupils to make a forecast about the success of a strategy.

The search for a solution or a way forward in an investigation, such as that explained in the Number Strings activity (see Chapter 4), requires the pupil to run and find connections between several mental models concurrently (Johnson-Laird, 1989; Payne, 1991), and the likelihood of success of the selected strategies or processes is determined. Not all likely ways forward in an investigation are certain to achieve useful results, so pupils need to be able to consider and evaluate all of the possible alternatives. Vosniadou (2002), who worked with children problem-solving in science, found that pupils will usually only run or select one mental model (strategy) in order to predict a likely solution. While limiting the opportunity for new learning, this singular selection enables teachers to focus on providing specific scaffolds that will support more novice mathematicians to consider other mental models that will carry them forward in the activity.

But Johnson-Laird (1989) and later Edwards-Leis (2013a) found that pupils who were more successful in determining possible solutions to problem situations were running various mental models simultaneously to make predictions about the solution's success. This synchronicity of mental model retrieval and running is very useful and characterizes pupils who have stored their knowledge in connected ways, enabling them to retrieve relevant procedures and knowledge at the critical times so that the application of strategy results in successful outcomes. The network of related understanding that Henderson and Tallman (2006) suggest is so beneficial for addressing novel problems can only be developed if children are exposed to a variety of experiences that allow them to see, think, apply and evaluate those experiences.

Not all of the strategies that a pupil will select will be successful in providing a way forward in an inquiry. The testing of the prediction means that mental models that don't quite fit will either be discarded because they are of no use as they are or will be manipulated in order to incorporate the new information emerging from the investigative process. This assimilation process is what Piaget (1970) explained as being so necessary to the construction of individual knowledge. Holyoak (1991) provides some interesting views on how pupils complete complex tasks, suggesting that while the individual is running simultaneous mental models to address a problem, they are switching between the alternatives, and this is often unconscious. If the switching and testing of possible solutions is made conscious, the pupil can be made more aware of the diagnostic function that mental models enact when such evaluation is occurring, and this appraisal recognition is useful for greater metacognitive awareness and success.

Diagnosing the success of ways forward

Schemas become less useful when they fail to enable the individual to act successfully in a given situation. In the 'light switch' example, the failure to find a light switch necessitates a following action, and the individual will do one of three things: enter the room and decide to not locate a light switch and fumble in the dark; enter the room and run their 'dark room' mental model to locate a source of lighting; or give up and walk away from the room. The diagnostic function is useful if the individual decides that the importance of their need to find what they require in the dark room is such that illumination is essential to find a light source. The diagnostic function is, therefore, reliant on the individual understanding that they do not have sufficient information to act successfully at a given point but that they can retrieve or locate information that will enable them to have a greater opportunity to do so. Jonassen (2011) explained that while diagnosis is the identification of a cause or reason for something that has occurred, there is some understanding by the individual of the certainty that there are a limited number of causes available for a specific effect.

Ritchie, Tobin and Hook (1997) used the term 'perturbation' to explain the contradictions that an individual will feel when they have insufficient information to solve a problem or enact a strategy. This term is similar to Piaget's (1970) 'disequilibrium' and requires the individual to remodel existing mental models to incorporate new information or to establish new mental models when the phenomenon is novel and has little relation to previous experiences. Gaining new information or learning new concepts, procedures or propositions often requires scaffolded support from a more knowledgeable other, reflecting Vygotsky's (1978, p. 8) Zone of Proximal Development (ZPD), in which the individual is supported "a little beyond" what they know in order to learn. Mental models are essential structures for this sponsored learning that enable the individual to not only gain new knowledge but also develop greater metacognitive awareness. Fundamentally, a pupil will become self-diagnosing throughout a school day if they are being constantly challenged to think or act beyond what they believe themselves capable of doing. If they are not being challenged, then in essence, they are simply replaying mental models or rehearsing their understanding and knowledge in order to store knowledge more securely. Constant retrieval and running is important for the development of long-term memory, but exposing pupils to novel and challenging situations is also integral to learning and the application of what is known to that which is not known.

When a pupil realizes that they do not have sufficient understanding, or mental models, to accomplish a task, then having some clarity about what to do next is essential, or frustration may encourage the pupil to withdraw from the learning experience. Poor behaviour in class can be attributed to not knowing what to do next, and providing pupils with strategies that enable them to act in such situations is necessary, particularly in mathematical activities. Novices require much more support

The functions of thinking

both to diagnose the success or failure of their predictions and to take control of their subsequent actions in order to have autonomy in the classroom. Mental models also control individual behaviour (Henderson & Tallman, 2006) or action, and this is because they provide selections of options when individuals are faced with choice. The control function acts like the command section and manages the determination of what comes next.

Controlling what happens

We often take for granted that we have control over our actions and have responsibility for the choices that we make. Such understanding, therefore, makes it difficult at times to decipher the unruly behaviour of children in classrooms in which the learning activities are designed to be interesting, engaging and achievable. Much of the disruptive behaviour in classrooms can be attributed to the inability of pupils to access the learning space in order to engage purposefully, creatively and/or successfully with the experiences designed by teachers. Henderson and Tallman's (2006) study of librarians instructing pupils who were searching for information on the Internet clearly established that while teachers are conscious of running mental models, particularly when they may be teaching new concepts such as the use of search engines, this conscious thinking does not impede the unconscious running of a mental model. Teachers will retrieve and run mental models that they may have used in the past, particularly where pupils may be having difficulties understanding the processes or knowledge required to undertake an activity. Such response to a surprise event in the classroom engages what Schön (1983) describes as reflection-in-action, which entails a decisive change of approach to deal with a phenomenon that prevents the planned lesson from proceeding. However, a teacher's response to pupils may also be unconscious and unproductive, such as a remonstration about behaviour that does not progress learning or engagement in the activity.

Altering our response to stimuli such as poor behaviour from pupils can be quite difficult, and Seel and Strittmatter (1989) found that a subjective explanatory value is often attached to mental models because individuals will repeat negative or unproductive strategies time after time. They found that individuals are reluctant to abandon mental models once they have been stored or linked to other mental models unless strong perceptual data that illuminates the inconsistency is provided. My study (Edwards-Leis, 2013a) followed pupils working with robots, and one teach-back episode clearly demonstrated the serious impact that a reluctance to address ineffectual mental models had on a pupil's ability to move forward in investigations. When faced with an obvious error, a pupil I will name Jenny enacted her 'problem-solving strategy' of repeating the steps taken to programme the robot. Jenny deleted then restructured the programme, but the robot continued to do the opposite action to the one

27

she had programmed; it went backwards *instead* of forwards. She was confident at programming the computer but was not a confident robot 'builder' so did not rebuild the robot. Jenny's mental model of robot construction controlled her actions. Failure to enact the 'repeat the steps' strategy on the actual robot resulted in error. After three reprogramming attempts, the robot continued to go backwards instead of forwards. To the surprise of the 'pupil' she was teaching Jenny's final observation was that the robot had operated correctly and that it was time to move on to the next activity.

A flawed mental model of building robots controlled Jenny's actions; the problem *was* a construction one because the leads had been connected incorrectly. She believed she could diagnose the problem, but her action to apply strategies to correct an error was limited because of the controlling nature of her mental models. This experience was a "stultifying" one (Henderson & Tallman, 2006, p. 25) because it stalled Jenny's progress, creating a cognitive blister (Edwards-Leis, 2013b) because of the failure to facilitate an effective solution. This example reinforces the controlling nature of mental models because Jenny needed to be willing to recognize her avoidance of building robots and restructure the mental model to accommodate more successful attitudes and processes. This learning act in essence is a "call to adapt an ineffectual mental model" and "requires an individual to recognise, and then instantiate, the necessary blend of knowledge, beliefs, metacognition and control" (Edwards-Leis, 2013a, p. 33) to do so. Johnson-Laird (2008, p. 349) suggested that "unconscious inferences lead us to have an emotional tie to beliefs about things that are unseen", and while such beliefs are vital to us they can be "immune to reasoned argument" and "malign[ant]" because they inhibit us from relinquishing or examining them even if they clash with the facts before us. Sometimes pupils who stubbornly cling to ways of working need to have their beliefs exposed so they can be explored in a supported environment. What is important to understand is that mental models need to be generative in order that they create new knowledge (Newton, 1996), which in essence involves the creation of new mental models.

Communicating what we know

Mental models facilitate the mediation of understanding between individuals; they help us to interact with others. The act of sharing what we know means that we are distributing our mental models through some medium. The most common medium in a classroom will be through oral discourse, although writing what we know and think is leading practice in modern classrooms, where digital media means that interactive white boards aid distribution of ideas quickly to a large group. Anderson, Howe and Tolmie (1996) discussed the existence of a transitory mental model that can be jointly held by participants to the dialogue. What is interesting about this notion, given the number of individuals in a classroom in which a teacher may be demonstrating a

The functions of thinking

mathematical procedure, such as the written algorithm for adding to a class of children, is the rich diversity of the interpretation of the transitory model that must exist. A teacher may feel that she is presenting a conceptual model of addition, but her *individual way of presenting* the process will be considered alongside the actual process when shared with the pupils in her class. This affective influence of the individual on any communication of ideas imposes significant implications on how a teacher uses actions, vocabulary and even facial expressions to explain processes, because *all* of the information present in such a transitory mental model will be processed by the pupils in the classroom and assimilated idiosyncratically into their individual mental models. If the teacher frowned while showing the process, then it must be difficult to do!

Henderson and Tallman (2006, p. 47) highlighted the "collaborative critique" of a teacher's mental model that occurs when they communicate with pupils through language and other nuances such as their body language, posture, facial expression, and voice modulation. The strength of these non-verbal communicative traits is profound and contributes to how pupils will interact with the learning environment or task. Such affective attributes seem to be particularly important in subjects such as mathematics in which the inability to make progress in seemingly straightforward procedures such as addition or subtraction is prevalent even in adults who profess an inability to 'do maths'! *How* we teach is, therefore, as important as *what* we teach, because we communicate a great deal of information to pupils continually throughout the day.

One of the approaches for effective teaching in a connectionist way (Askew, 2012) is to use analogy (Gentner, 1998; Newton, 1996) because it is useful to communicate concepts to others by focusing on transferable characteristics of the analogy to the concept. Newton (1996) discussed how analogy involves mapping from one source structure to another structure, which is referred to as the target, sharing useful attributes relevant to the pupils. Teachers cover two types of analogy in Primary classrooms: simile and metaphor are useful analogies for children to explore and remember the connections between phenomena. Examples that are meaningful for children include similes such as 'as tall as a house' and metaphors like 'this classroom is a zoo'! Ideas are therefore communicated more clearly and colourfully, and any related understanding is more likely to be anchored more successfully to analogous structures within new or existing mental models.

Diagrams and graphical representations, like analogy, help secure more effective communication of ideas. Doyle, Radzicki and Trees (2008) found that using a variety of diagrams and matrices was useful in representing the change in mental models that occurred when individuals learned something new. Williamson (1999) likewise used concept maps to show the learning exhibited by pre-service teachers offering a structured graphical representation of arrangements of connected concepts within a domain of learning. Chang (2007) also used concept maps with pupils, asking them to

29

draw them while they were being asked *questions* about abstract ideas, and Ahlberg (2008) *confirmed* their effective use because both novices and experts in a domain will alter the mental models expressed through concept maps as they gain more expertise. For teachers wishing to establish what pupils know about certain areas of mathematics, concept map creation using diagrams and symbols as well as words provides a useful mechanism to test for existing knowledge before planning for subsequent activities. Gaining a better understanding of how mental models are stored in long-term memory and recalled to short-term or working memory for working during inquiries is of great interest to educators because such knowledge better equips them to design their pedagogy more effectively.

Memory mechanisms

Mental models are bimodal because they are cognitive structures that have the potential to be permanent in long-term memory but have a transient nature when run in working memory (Bagley & Payne, 2000; Hambrick & Engle, 2002). The capacity of working memory to deal with the active running of many mental models was discussed in the previous chapter, and the issue is a constant and relevant one for teachers who are wishing to design learning experiences that challenge pupils yet do not over-stretch their capacity to deal with multiple mental models being simultaneously run. So this function of mental models is a fundamental one and one often taken for granted by teachers who believe that if they teach a concept once in a connectionist and therefore memorable way then the pupils should retain it. But we realize that this is not the case, particularly when some testing regime requires pupils to regurgitate propositional knowledge or apply procedural knowledge in a novel situation such as would occur in solving problems.

But practising skills repetitively is useful and relevant to strengthening the links that relate the information in idiosyncratic ways by the individual. Fluency is a result of repetitive and successful application of knowledge and is, quite rightly, one of the aims of the national curriculum of England and Wales (DfE, 2013). We only have to realize how our own memories of past events are triggered by some minor act, smell, sound or touch to appreciate the multitude of information stored over time from our rich and often repeated experiences in mental models. Such multifarious information helps secure knowledge and aid the retrieval of it when required, signalling implications for the connectionist approach (Askew, 2012) to learning mathematics that is advocated. Paying attention to what is to be learned through the derivation or reconstruction of a mental model and therefore what needs to be retrieved from long-term memory or the environment so as to enact a successful strategy in an inquiry is a complex task that, often, only experts in a field can manage. Therefore, the preparation of pupils so that they can become experts is an important goal for teachers.

30

Moving forward

I taught in a London Primary school where I delighted in spending time with a class of curious Year Four children. Most mornings the school community came together for an assembly in which various activities including singing, sharing of work and the occasional presentation by a teacher of a shared value that was explored with interesting visual aids and an intriguing story engaged everyone. For the most part these morning sessions were very enjoyable and contributed to a sense of school cohesiveness. On the mornings when there was no assembly, I would prepare Power-Point slides (see Figure 2.1) that had 16 images on them in a square grid. I would ask the children (and teaching assistants, who enjoyed the activity too!) to concentrate on the images for 15 seconds, and then I would blacken the screen before requesting that

Figure 2.1 Example of the picture grid for morning games

they record all of the images they could remember. While seemingly a bit of a game, this activity became a valued part of the children's (and adults') learning in which meta-cognitive awareness was the vanguard.

Once everyone had written down the images they had remembered, we would look at the grid again and tick the ones that were correct. This 'marking' was not a formal assessment of memory but a way to encourage the children to share their *method* of remembering. Some pupils had few strategies, usually only the repetition approach in which the names of the items were repeated. Others had some useful and interesting strategies such as linking or chunking similar objects (ball, sun, orange) or creating a quick sentence or narrative (I used a pencil to draw a robot and a doll in the book) to make a story sequence. I explained that Miller (1956) had established some understanding about how many discrete pieces of information an individual could hold in their working memory at one time. The equation '7 plus or minus 2' pieces of information (Miller, 1956) became a familiar mantra in the classroom. I also likened our mind's working memory to a school desk: the more similar items you can stack together, the more you can keep on your desk so that you can work easily. This metaphor was easily understood by the pupils, and many of them started to use different strategies that other pupils had described in the hope of being able to remember more items. Indeed, they were encouraged to try new approaches.

Early adoption, however, did not ensure success! Many pupils found that their scores were worse when they first tried to link 'sun, ball, orange' and the 'pencil and the book': their *efforts* to chunk similar items or *create a narrative* were taking up some of their working memory, thereby reducing how many items they remembered. However, we discussed that new strategies required effort and time to learn, thereby explaining the need for patience with ourselves as new approaches were rehearsed and refined. This *time for learning* is something children, and adults, can forget: gaining new knowledge, regardless of the type that it is, takes time and practice, so being willing to persevere in the face of reduced effectiveness takes understanding of what the learning process entails for each of us as individuals. The development of the Mental Model Mode followed the experiences of these pupils at this time when they were in Year Four and again two years later when several of them participated in a research project on its use in design and technology and mathematics problem situations.

The Mental Model Mode: a way to explain the functions of mental modelling

A research project was held in 2012 to explore how well the Mental Model Mode (see Figure 2.2) matched the mental modelling functions that occurred when pupils were engaged in solving problems. The pupils in the project were in Year Six and eager

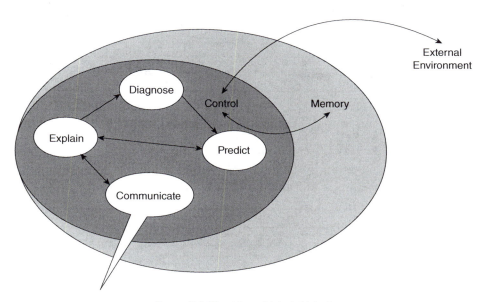

Figure 2.2 The Mental Model Mode

to undertake the challenges I had set for them. The research followed BERA (2011) ethical guidelines. I designed two sets of activities for them: one problem was ill defined (Jonassen, 2011) and required them to design an artefact to meet a specified brief, while the other set was well structured (Jonassen, 2011) and engaged them in a series of mathematical activities. The mathematical activities required them to interpret worded challenges, to adopt logical approaches and deal with spatial puzzles. The children were filmed during the 15 minutes they were given to complete each of the two activities. Later on the same day as the activity they had completed, they were interviewed while watching the videos of their efforts. Stimulated Recall Methodology was used to gain the thoughts of each, thereby allowing the functions being used to solve the problems to be externalized and subsequently analyzed.

Three functions dominated the well-structured (Jonassen, 2011) problem-solving domain of mathematics that the children engaged with: explaining (43%), diagnosing (26%) and predicting (18%) were the most frequently used functions by the children. Unsurprisingly the function most commonly used by the participants was explaining. An early researcher in Mental Model Theory was Johnson-Laird (1983, p. 3), who described an individual's attempt to understand their world as constructing "models of it in their mind", and this action was clearly seen by the pupils as they worked through the activities. He later described mental models as "the end result of perception and of understanding a description" (Johnson-Laird, 2008, p. 428). Understanding is externalized through explanation and is different to simply being able to describe something. Johnson-Laird (2008, p. 177) enlightened our understanding of this function when he stated "we can describe an event without understanding it, but we cannot explain an event unless we have some putative understanding of it". We explain through our actions and words including structures of language necessary for the domain (for example 'adding' and 'subtracting' are terms used to describe specific procedures in mathematics), concepts and vocabulary.

The Mode in Figure 2.2 shows how the functions operate when we are working on finding solutions and were clearly expressed by the pupils in the study described. The explanatory function, shown by the ellipse *explain*, helps us to understand and select strategies by "facilitating cognitive and physical interactions with the environment, with others, and with artefacts" (Henderson & Tallman, 2006, p. 25). *Explain* has arrows pointing to *predict, diagnose* and *communicate* because our explanation of what we know, expect to do or see as a result of an action lead us forward in the activity to other functions such as *making predictions, diagnosing outcomes* and, at times, *communicating results.*

The predictive function, shown by the ellipse *predict*, enables the pupil to make an educated guess or prediction about how a strategy might solve the problem. It has arrows coming from and going to *explain* because once an aspect of a problem is understood, the individual will make a prediction of the success of a selected strategy. It also has an arrow coming from *diagnose* because once an individual has diagnosed the quality of their knowledge to make a prediction, they will do so. The *predict* function is what really differentiates mental models from other cognitive structures such as schema because its presence in the problem-solving process accounts for novel situations for which we have no stored schema.

The diagnostic function, shown by the ellipse *diagnose*, engages the budding metacognitive awareness and associated understanding that a pupil is developing because it requires a testing of both the outcome of the strategy and its perceived success in comparison to the requirement of the task. It has an arrow moving forward to *predict*, indicating that the individual will move to make a prediction of the success of a strategy once it has been evaluated as being supported by the relevant knowledge necessary for application. A pupil needs to have a reasonable idea of what a 'good' answer will look like in order to diagnose the closeness of their solution to the *right* one. The function *diagnose* also relies on the pupil having an understanding that they may be working with an incomplete mental model; they may need to seek information or material from elsewhere in order to reach a reasonable solution.

Memory continues to play a pivotal role in the process of mental modelling and is shown on the diagram in Figure 2.2 as the largest ellipse. It forms the background for all of the mental modelling because it contains the long-term memory, in which information required for retrieval for application to the activity may be stored. Not only does the pupil have to be able to work effectively in their working memory space,

The functions of thinking

shown by the ellipse with the *control* function, but they need to able to retrieve the appropriate knowledge that is embedded in existing mental models from long-term memory in order to complete a task. This bimodality (Edwards-Leis, 2013a) of mental models is of interest. We retrieve mental models as products from our long-term memory, run them as processes in our working memory, then store them once again in our long-term memory as a new or remodelled product after completion of the problem-solving episode. How well they are subsequently stored is also important for future retrieval.

The control function, shown in the second-largest ellipse as *control*, has arrows moving between its ellipse, which represents the individual's working memory where the processing activity is taking place, and the *memory* function where mental models are stored. The *control* function also has arrows going to and from the external environment because the individual, through control via an evaluation of their ability to *explain, diagnose* and *predict* while mental modelling will extract information required for the successful completion of the activity from an external source. External sources may be other individuals such as teachers or information in texts, on the Internet or on wall charts. Sometimes the individual is required to *communicate* with others, particularly other pupils in their class. When an individual communicates, they create a *Transitory Mental Model*, which links one individual's mental model space to that of another. The transitory nature of mental models occurs when more than one person is working simultaneously on an activity with another person. Their discourse, the dialogue, ideas and explanations they share sit between them while the activity is in progress. Once the activity is complete, each individual takes from it what they see as relevant and true and stores it in their individual mental models. If you asked two people who shared a learning experience to explain what they did, each would provide a similar yet idiosyncratic episode due to the individual nature of interpretation. This is an important aspect of learning that teachers need to keep reviewing: different views do not represent a binary, but they do represent a clear example of the power of mental models to influence our perception of a phenomenon and our understanding of its relevance.

Mental modelling is not complex: we do it every day. Breaking down the functions that occur when we are mental modelling is useful when planning for stimulating mathematics lessons that help children learn and remember. Primary school teachers are experts at presenting pupils with rich learning experiences that have the contexts that better enable the network of related understandings necessary for both the effective completion of challenging activities and the efficient storage of knowledge. Askew (2012) refers to connectionism as the means of ensuring that what is learnt is meaningful at the time when it should be remembered. Giving lessons in imaginative and fecund environments and contexts ensures the network or relatedness of memories are more likely to result in more secure storing of knowledge after a rich and rewarding exploration of the event.

35

The Mode Typology

Freire (1972, p. 81) suggested that "all authentic education investigates thinking", and the Mode provides a structure that will enable teachers and their pupils to explore their own thought processes while engaged in thinking, particularly in solving problems or mathematical investigations. It helps to clarify an individual's *way* of thinking and to externalize the cognitive processes for a rich discourse between teacher and pupil or among pupils themselves. Individuals, and therefore the pupils in your class, do not all think the same way, although there are similarities in the processes of thinking. The Mode can be used in classrooms to understand, diagnose, remediate and celebrate through sharing how pupils cognitively navigate pathways through learning experiences and has the potential to give some structure to the "common reflection and action" (Freire, 1972, p. 44) necessary for co-intentional education that most teachers aim for in their Primary classrooms.

Guidance is, however, still necessary so that teachers and pupils can work together effectively in problem-rich situations. Fry (2009) suggested that it is necessary for individuals to become purposeful interrogators of self, arguing that reflective interrogation is part of a re-educative process that encourages actions and outcomes that are not useful to be eliminated from our regular practice. While his focus was on sustainability, it could be argued that teaching pupils in Primary school to be efficient and effective interrogators of themselves will arm them well for their futures as Secondary pupils and as adults. If pupils have learned that they are not as good at problem solving in mathematics as they think they should be, then not only do they need to learn new skills, but they also need to un-learn the attitudes that will hinder the acquisition of new knowledge. Overcoming persistent difficulties in mathematical investigations and problem solving therefore requires not just the adoption of a new strategy or schema but a deliberate and sustained interrogation of mental models so that pupils can reshape their thinking.

Jonassen (2011), who has done extensive research into problem solving in many domains, recognized that there was not a great deal of helpful research on metacognitive prompting in problem solving. He suggested that what has been done shows "when pupils self-regulate their learning by identifying their own knowledge deficits and then ask questions that remediate those deficits, they learn more effectively" (Jonassen, 2011, p. 292). Such a process obviously requires guidance and training by teachers who can facilitate a logical and sequential approach that suits all pupils and that can be adapted individually to meet specific deficits and strengths. There has been significant research (Graesser, Baggett & Williams, 1996; Graesser & Olde, 2003; Graesser, Person & Huber, 1992; King, 1991; Palinscar & Brown, 1984) into the types of questions that can prompt pupils when problem solving, recognizing that "questions are asked when people experience cognitive disequilibrium while solving problems, which is triggered by contradictions, anomalies, obstacles, salient contrasts, and uncertainty" (Jonassen, 2011, p. 285). Therefore, the Mode Typology has been developed to contain mostly questions with additional prompts that can focus the learner's attention on the next step to take to deal with obstacles in the investigative and problem-solving processes.

More of the Mode Typology will be introduced in the next chapter, in which we explore approaches to mathematical problem solving and investigations. A unique approach that provides a structure upon which the Mode and Mode Typology can sit will be explained. This supported approach to the process of inquiry will then be demonstrated through some unique activities that appear in the following chapters, thereby providing a rich source of material for you to use in your classrooms. At the very least the Mode Typology provides an integral guide for teachers to use to support their questioning and prompting in the Primary classroom.

References

Ahlberg, M. (2008). *Practical methods and techniques of knowledge representation in particular those related to concept mapping and mind mapping: History, theoretical background, software, and comparison table.* Retrieved August 30, 2009, from http://itech1.coe.uga.edu/itforum/paper109/Ahlberg_manuscript.pdf

Anderson, T., Howe, C., & Tolmie, A. (1996). Interaction and mental models of physics phenomena: Evidence from dialogues between learners. In J. Oakhill & A. Garnham (Eds.), *Mental models in cognitive science* (pp. 247–273). East Sussex, UK: Psychology Press.

Askew, M. (2012). *Transforming primary mathematics.* Oxon, UK: Routledge.

Bagley, T., & Payne, S. (2000). Long-term memory for spatial and temporal mental models includes construction processes and model structure. *The Quarterly Journal of Experimental Psychology, 53A*(2), 479–512.

British Educational Research Association (BERA). (2011). *Ethical guidelines for educational research.* London, UK: BERA. [Online] Available at: https://www.bera.ac.uk/wp-content/uploads/2014/02/BERA-Ethical-Guidelines-2011.pdf?noredirect=1

Chang, S. N. (2007). Externalising students' mental models through concept maps. *Journal of Biological Education, 41*(3), 107–112.

Department for Education (2013). *The national curriculum for England and Wales.* London, UK: DfE.

Doyle, J., Radzicki, M., & Trees, W. (2008). Measuring change in mental models of complex systems. In H. Qudrat-Ullah, J. M. Spector, & P. I. Davidsen (Eds.),

Complex decision making: Theory and practice (pp. 269–294). New York, NY: Springer-Verlag Press.

Edwards-Leis, C. E. (2013a). *Understanding learning through Mental Model Theory.* Saarbrücken, Germany: LAP Lambert Academic Publishing.

Edwards-Leis, C. E. (2013b). Knowing where the shoe pinches: Using the Mental Model Mode to understand how Primary pupils an design intelligently. In *Technology education for the future: A play on sustainability, PATT27 Conference* (pp. 141–148). Christchurch, NZ: University of Waikato.

Freire, P. (1972). *Pedagogy of the oppressed.* London, UK: Penguin Books.

Fry, T. (2009). *Design futuring: Sustainability, ethics and new practice.* New York, NY: Berg.

Gentner, D. (1998). Analogy. In W. Bechtel & G. Graham (Eds.), *A companion to cognitive science* (pp. 107–113). Oxford: Blackwell.

Graesser, A. C., Baggett, W., & Williams, K. (1996). Question-driven explanatory reasoning. *Applied Cognitive Psychology, 10*(7), S17–S31.

Graesser, A. C., & Olde, B. A. (2003). How does one know whether a person understands a device? The quality of the questions the person asks when the device breaks down. *Journal of Educational Psychology, 95*(3), 524–536.

Graesser, A. C., Person, N. K., & Huber, J. D. (1992). Mechanisms that generate questions. In T. E. Lauer, E. Peacock, & A. C. Graesser (Eds.), *Questions and information systems* (pp. 167–187). Hillsdale, NJ: Lawrence Erlbaum.

Hambrick, D. Z., & Engle, R. W. (2002). Effects of domain knowledge, working memory capacity, and age on cognitive performance: An investigation of the knowledge-is-power hypothesis. *Cognitive Psychology, 44*, 339–387.

Henderson, L., & Tallman, J. (2006). *Stimulated recall and mental models.* Lanham, MD: Scarecrow Press, Inc.

Holyoak, K. J. (1991). Symbolic connectionism: Toward third-generation theories of expertise. In K. A. Ericsson & J. Smith (Eds.), *Toward a general theory of expertise* (pp. 301–335). Cambridge, UK: Cambridge University Press.

Johnson-Laird, P. N. (1983). *Mental models: Towards a cognitive science of language, inference, and consciousness.* Cambridge: Cambridge University Press and Cambridge, MA: Harvard University Press.

Johnson-Laird, P. N. (1989). Mental models. In M. I. Posner (Ed.), *Foundations of cognitive science.* (pp. 469–499). Cambridge, MA: MIT Press.

Johnson-Laird, P. N. (2008). *How we reason.* Oxford, UK: Oxford University Press.

Jonassen, D. H. (2011). *Learning to solve problems: A handbook for designing problem-solving learning environments.* New York, NY: Routledge.

King, A. (1991). Effects of training in strategic questioning on children's problem solving performance. *Journal of Educational Psychology, 83*(3), 307–317.

Miller, G. (1956). The magical number seven, plus or minus two: Some limits on our capacity for processing information. *Psychological Review, 63*, 81–97.

Newton, D. (1996). Causal situations in science: A model for supporting understanding. In R. Saljo (Ed.), *Learning and instruction* (Vol. 6(3), pp. 201–217). Great Britain: Elsevier Science Ltd.

Norman, D. A. (1983). Some observations on mental models. In D. Gentner & A. L. Stevens (Eds.), *Mental models* (pp. 7–14). Hillsdale, NJ: Lawrence Erlbaum.

Palinscar, A. S., & Brown, A. L. (1984). Reciprocal teaching of comprehension-fostering and comprehension-monitoring activities. *Cognition and Instruction, 2*(2), 117–175.

Payne, S. (1991). Display-based action at the user interface. *International Journal of Man-Machine Studies, 35*, 275–289.

Piaget, J. (1970). *The science of education and the psychology of the child.* New York, NY: Orion Press.

Pring, R. (2010). *Philosophy of educational research.* London, UK: Continuum.

Ritchie, S. M., Tobin, K., & Hook, K. S. (1997). Teaching referents and the warrants used to test the viability of students' mental models: Is there a link? *Journal of Research in Science Training, 34*(3), 223–238.

Schön, D. A. (1983). *The reflective practitioner: How professionals think in action.* New York, NY: Basic Books.

Seel, N. M., & Strittmatter, P. (1989). Presentation of information by media and its effect on mental models. In J. R. Levin & H. Mandl (Eds.), *Knowledge acquisition from text and pictures* (pp. 37–57). Amsterdam, The Netherlands: Elsevier Science Publications.

Vosniadou, S. (2002). Mental models in conceptual development. In L. Magnani & N. Nersessian (Eds.), *Model-based reasoning: Science, technology, values.* New York, NY: Kluwer Academic Press.

Vygotsky, L. S. (1978). *Mind in society.* Cambridge, MA: Harvard University Press.

Williamson, J. W. (1999). *Mental models of teaching: Case study of selected pre-service teachers enrolled in an introductory educational technology course* (Doctoral dissertation). University of Georgia, Athens, GA.

Ways to problem solve and investigate
Scaffolds and structures

Being playful and creative

There was a great loss to society when Christopher Zeeman (1925–2016) died. He was a pioneering mathematician famous for several texts including *Catastrophe Theory* (1977) and *Gyroscopes and Boomerangs* (1989). He also saw the value of play in learning mathematics and suggested that one of the better ways to engage children was to find something playful in it and then play! Zeeman also saw mathematics as both an art and a science, because sometimes you invent it and at others you discover it. He suggested, "you have to invent maths to get a solution to a problem but, in the process, I often discover a whole lot more which I didn't expect" (Arnot, 2005, pp. 20–21). Haylock (2010, p. 16) also sees mathematics as a creative endeavour in which "flexibility and imaginative thinking can lead to interesting outcomes or fresh avenues to explore for the curious mind". But such flexible, creative and investigative approaches to mathematics take time, and Askew (2012) challenges the orthodoxy of the packaging of mathematical learning into a lesson. He suggests leaving problems unresolved at the end of a lesson and returning to them the following day is beneficial for learning. We would suggest that incubation and pondering time are valuable, and these approaches, while 'messy' for some teachers, actually enrich the dialogue between teacher and learner, and perhaps between child and parent, as children have the opportunity to take intriguing problems home with them to share with the family. Therefore, a significant way to develop mathematical reasoning is to create time for it and thereby free the constraints that were mentioned in Chapter 2. Being playful, creative and discovering new ideas takes time, but what a significant investment.

Ways to problem solve and investigate

Is there a skill set?

One of the major questions many teachers ask is what types of inquiries do children need to be able to do successfully? Is there a particular skill set to be acquired and applied? While there seems to be a significant number of texts published about problem solving and investigating, each proposes a novel route and offers different approaches for teachers to use. There is also no clear answer to these questions in the latest curriculum (DfE, 2013), although it does contain indicators of practice throughout the years. However, a major indicator for supporting inquiry in mathematics, particularly in England and Wales, is the presence of reasoning and problem solving, where the expectation is that children will be able to "reason mathematically by following a line of enquiry, conjecturing relationships and generalizations, and developing an argument, justification or proof using mathematical language" (DfE, 2013, p. 3). There is no separate strand for problem solving in the curriculum document because the presence of problem solving is embedded throughout the different areas as written in the statutory requirements for each level. Sometimes the expectations are very specific and at other times less so. The final point of the statutory requirements in several sections advises that *pupils should be taught to solve problems that involve all of the above*, indicating that the retention of knowledge of discrete concepts, facts and skills is insufficient and that understanding *how* this knowledge is to be applied for problem solving is a mandated part of the curriculum.

Guidance for teachers in the Upper Key Stage 2 section provides an explanation for problem-solving expectations in a general sense in the preamble, where it says "at this stage, pupils should develop their ability to solve a wider range of problems including increasingly complex properties of numbers and arithmetic, and problems demanding efficient written and mental methods of calculation" (DfE, 2013, p. 30). More detail is subsequently provided in which learners are required to "solve problems involving multiplication and division including using their knowledge of factors and multiples, squares and cubes" or "solve problems involving multiplication and division, including scaling by simple fractions and problems involving simple rates" (DfE, 2013, p. 32). So the requirements do become quite specific with processes such as *scaling* to be included. But where does this guidance leave teachers who are seeking to provide opportunities to develop mathematical reasoning through problem solving and investigations? Should teachers be planning to *include discrete* problem solving and investigative activities, or should they be planning to *incorporate the processes* of problem solving and investigating in their planning for mathematics? Should they adopt a 'bolt-on' or 'build-in' approach?

We suggest doing both. They are both an essential part of developing pupils' mathematical learning. Problem-solving and investigative activities provide potentially purposeful, meaningful and intriguing opportunities for the learner. We believe that is it is the teacher's intention for the focus of learning that identifies the distinct difference and makes both essential.

In *discrete*, 'bolt-on' problem-solving and investigative activities, pupils are provided with an opportunity to select, use and apply their knowledge and understanding (*mathematical content*) in a unique problem space. So in their planning teachers would ensure that pupils have a particular predictable set of mathematical content that enables them to engage with the activity. Further, for the pupils' learning experiences to be successful, teaching must focus on the development strategies and thinking *processes* presented/provided by the challenge.

In contrast, in a more *integrated*, 'built-in' approach the problem-solving and investigative activities present/provide opportunities for pupils to explore their known mathematical content in order to broaden and strengthen their mathematical knowledge and understanding. Teaching focuses on the development of conceptual understanding and discovery of new relationships through the *process* of problem solving and investigating. Both develop mastery by planning for fluency, problem solving and mathematical reasoning, but in fundamentally different and symbiotic ways.

Table 3.1 shows the diagram of the categories of inquiry where problem solving and investigating are seen as *bolted-on* experiences and solving problems is a *built-in* approach.

Typically *bolt-on* problem-solving and investigative activities are bigger and may take place over a lesson and even extend over several lessons or continue beyond the classroom. The emphasis is on the application of mathematical *fluency* in order to develop *problem and mathematical reasoning*. Whereas *built-in* activities are smaller and use *problem solving* and *mathematical reasoning* to develop *fluency*. Both contribute to planning for mastery.

Table 3.1 Bolt-on and built-in approaches

Bolt-on	• Planning for bigger activities, which may extend over a lesson or over several lessons, even continuing beyond the classroom.
	• Teaching emphasis on the application of mathematical *content* in order to develop mathematical *processes*.
	• Learning opportunities increase, evaluate and refine problem-solving and investigative processes through the selection and application of knowledge and understanding
Built-in	• Planning for smaller activities, which may be used as extension tasks for the latter part of a lesson or topic.
	• Teaching emphasis on engagement of mathematical *processes* in order to apply mathematical *content*.
	• Learning opportunities to develop conceptual understanding and relationships discovered through the process of problem solving and investigating.

It would seem that the advice found in such documents as the *Independent Review of Mathematics Teaching in Early Years Settings and Primary Schools* (Williams, 2008) and *Mathematics: Made to Measure* (Ofsted, 2012) has been addressed in the new curriculum. Williams (2008, p. 62) stressed the need "to strengthen teaching that challenges and enables children to use and apply mathematics more often, and more effectively, than is presently the case in many schools". The focus of the aims on mastery in understanding, retaining and applying knowledge in the new curriculum document is clear. But a more recent report by Ofsted (2012, p. 9), *Mathematics: Made to Measure*, is worrying because it reported while schools were aware of the necessity of improving learners' problem-solving and investigative skills that "such activities were rarely integral to learning except in the best schools where they were at the heart of learning mathematics". Ofsted's (2012) reference to activities that are "integral to learning" would indicate that effective teaching (and therefore planning) is not just about the *type* of problem-solving activities to include but the *approach* to problem solving that needs to be clarified. Therefore, a skill set or list of types of problems is not really beneficial because it would reduce the culture of investigation to a checklist or, more dangerously, to an acronym in which all problem-solving activities can be covered referring to a single process. Jenny, who in a previous chapter was shown to be adept at following a recipe for problem solving (repeat your steps!), was unable to solve a relatively simple problem due to her controlling mental model, which was embedded in a recipe of what to do if something goes wrong.

Challenging convention

There is significant criticism of quite popular approaches to problem solving in Primary mathematics that is enlightening to explore. Barmby, Bolden and Thompson (2014) reinforce Askew's (2012) challenge to the orthodox 'delivery' of problem-solving activities within the constraint of a mathematics lesson. They suggest that problem solving takes time and that the national curriculum can actually constrain teachers if they don't start thinking conceptually about mathematics rather than as an unchanging body of knowledge to be taught. Barmby et al. (2014) explore a variety of types and approaches including Orton and Frobisher's (1999) three types (routine, environmental, process) and Bransford and Steing's (1984 cited in Nickerson, 1994, p. 96) IDEAL (identify the problem, define and present the problem, explore possible strategies, act on the strategies, look back and evaluate the effect of the activities). They are most scathing of the RUCSAC (read, understand/underline, choose, solve, answer, check) and QUACK (question, understand/underline, approximate, calculate, know) approaches that seem to be popular in many Primary classrooms as being of little use to learners who are confident or for those who have little confidence due to the fact that neither offers a route back into the problem if the learner becomes 'stuck'.

More criticism for some tokenistic approaches to problem solving comes from Fairclough (2011), who critiques Burton's (1986) popular book on problem solving. Fairclough (2011, p. 87) suggests,

> early in the development of problem solving in the mathematics classroom, Leone Burton stated that problem solving cannot be taught. An interesting statement in a book containing a wealth of interesting problems for children to solve, each problem requiring, according to Burton, no more skills than the child already has.

However, this criticism may be quite harsh given Burton's focus on taking advantage of a child's natural curiosity, which could be instrumental in promoting Zeeman's idea of 'play'. She also suggested the development of clear questioning techniques, present in her *entry, attack, review* procedure, which we would support as being fundamental for teacher and pupil in their quest to develop what Zeeman referred to as opportunities for 'inventing maths' and discovering something new. So while some teachers, particularly those new to the craft, may wish simply to be told *what to do* to get children engaged in problem solving, any one way can be critiqued and found wanting. Perhaps looking more deeply into what happens when we problem solve, investigating the processes of thinking that are essential to learning, may provide a more holistic approach that can be intuitively massaged to account for both the teacher's idiosyncratic ways of understanding and problem solving and the learners' rich variety of anomalous mental models.

Back to basics?

The predominant theme in most texts and websites that focus on developing children's mathematical problem-solving skills is the need for context. One of the earliest and most useful models upon which to provide a context for problem solving is Polya's (1957) model, which has four basic steps:

1 Understand the nature of the problem.
2 Draw a plan to solve the problem.
3 Try the plan.
4 Monitor the outcome of the plan.

While the model seems simple, the thinking and action that are necessary for each step of the model to be achieved successfully are quite complex, and hence the challenges that teachers face to provide opportunities for useful and successful problem solving in Primary mathematics. Perhaps Jonassen's (2011) discussion on problem schemas may help to illuminate clearer pathways for teachers to follow when they consider problem-solving activities or investigations for children. Such an approach may also make the need to embed problem solving and application of knowledge to areas of learning in the national curriculum more logical.

The development of a schematic approach to problem solving rests on the assumption that conceptual understanding of the structure of the problem is essential before any successful attempt can be made to solve it. Problem schemas, according to Rumelhart and Ortony (1977), who introduced the concept, include information that is both semantic and situational about the problem associated with the processes for solving that type of problem. Later, Riley, Greeno and Heller (1983) suggested that not only do problems vary according to their semantic structure, which involve combinations of values, but also by the location of the unknown quantity. Jonassen (2011) suggested that some of the simplest story problems from Primary mathematics allow us to understand these terms and what they mean for developing a variety of approaches to problem solving. He proposed that the simplest type of mathematical story problems include "combine, change, and compare problems" (Jonassen, 2011, p. 242). The quantity that is unknown can then vary among the problems where in one it may be the result, in another the amount of change or in another the starting quantity in the problem. Teachers would be familiar with all of these problem types and use them in examples such as:

> *Unknown as a result in a combine problem:* Jon has three oranges. Ken gave Jon three more oranges. How many apples does Jon have in the end?
>
> *Unknown as the amount of change in a compare problem:* Jon has four oranges. Ken has some too. Altogether they have nine oranges. How many oranges does Ken have?

In each aspect of the compare problem there are different structural elements. Each has a specification (Jon/Ken/Jon + Ken), an object (oranges) and a quantity (4/?/9). Jonassen (2011) warns of children memorizing questions and mimicking problem-solving procedures without understanding the concepts behind the questions. He suggests that children should also be able to identify the different aspects of a problem and assign it some kind of conceptual model based on its relationship within the domain. Such generic propositions, in mathematics, include "quantity (number, some, how many), possession (have, give), compare (more than, less than), and time (past, beginning, then)" (Jonassen, 2011, p. 243). Children who develop robust problem-solving skills are able to do so because they have been able to arrange the structural elements and the generic propositions into a coherent conceptual model. While it is important to revisit these processes through repetition, it is important to realize that children are revisiting the conceptual development of the problem-solving model and not just memorizing a process.

Psychologists Pretz, Naples and Sternberg (2003) approached the problem-solving process in an iterative way that, while not specifically promoting the development of a problem-solving schema or a conceptual model, offers the opportunity for the learner to evaluate their progress throughout the activity. They suggest a cycle that includes:

- Recognizing or identifying the problem;
- Defining or representing the problem mentally;
- Developing a solution strategy;
- Organizing knowledge about the problem;
- Allocating mental and physical resources for solving the problem;
- Monitoring progress towards the goal; and,
- Evaluating the solution, possibly leading to a new problem.

There is a healthy lack of acronyms with Pretz et al.'s (2003) process that have been expressed here by us as verbs (recognizing, defining, developing) due to their being more closely linked to actions that learners would undertake when they are thinking mathematically. The approach to creating verbs to express what we do makes sense, and Anderson and Krathwohl (2001) underwent a similar process when they revised Bloom's (1956) taxonomy. They found that using Bloom's higher levels (e.g. analyzing, evaluating, creating) when prompting children with questions helped them to become better problem solvers. When they asked the pupils to also use diagrams and words as well as numbers, they found the pupils were better able to explain their thought processes. Anderson and Krathwohl (2001) also created actions (e.g. planning, devising, making) to accompany their higher-order thinking terms, and these are very useful for teachers when planning activities to engage pupils in mathematical problem solving. But two major questions are lurking, something like Krylov's elephant in the museum (in this case the classroom!): when do you prompt children during the problem-solving process, and what questions do you ask at those points that will move their thinking forward rather than giving them the answer?

Arming children to investigate!

The taxonomies that have been produced over time to guide Primary teachers in their planning for including problem solving in mathematics lessons are useful because they are a reference tool that reminds teachers to seek inspiration when they find themselves relying on tried-and-trusted methods to solve problems rather than being more diverse in their range of approaches. Many websites are also now available that can offer teachers immediate access to significant assistance in their planning for problem solving (see NRICH and National Centre for Excellence in the Teaching of Mathematics [NCETM] sites for inspiration). It is undeniable that children require an understanding of a broad range of approaches to solving problems, and the introduction of such methods can be both a blessing and also problematic. The introduction and practice of methods of problem solving often take over the classroom activities, and children do not get to actually use the approaches in real investigations. This practice pedagogy is similar to practising for a game of netball but never getting to play an actual game.

Questions have been raised about the value of 'domain knowledge', although there is significant agreement that a learner's prior domain knowledge is a strong determiner of success in problem solving. But much of the research in this field was conducted using well-structured problems (Jonassen, 2011), and it is not just about the quantity of knowledge that a learner has but the quality of that knowledge. Jonassen (2011, p. 20) advised that to solve any problem, the learner must "possess better-integrated conceptual frameworks for domain knowledge that accommodate multiple perspectives, methods, and solutions". Vosniadou (2002) suggests that to enable learners to develop the integrated conceptual frameworks necessary for robust problem solving teachers should challenge them with conflicting information. In other words, teachers need to disturb learners' equilibrium with conceptually oriented instruction; learners need to be aware that they may not know all that they need to know to solve a problem, because domain knowledge, regardless of the domain, is seldom sufficient to solve real problems.

The Mode Typology is part of a framework that provides a selection of questions and prompts that enable teachers and learners to find ways through problem-solving situations when faced with what we call cognitive blisters or those times when the next steps on the learning journey are stalled due to lack of ideas or knowledge on what to do next (Edwards-Leis, 2013). Sometimes you need to take your shoes off and check for the blisters that are hindering the steps necessary for the journey. We also have outlined an approach to problem solving that shows how the different stages of problem solving can be supported by the typology. The Mode Typology adds significantly to this method by providing teachers with key questions and prompts at specific points so as to engage children in real opportunities to think deeply and productively about what they know, what might happen next and what they might need to try in order to move forward in their investigation. A review of the requirements of the current curriculum in England and how the use of the Mode Typology can assist teachers in the development of mastery in their mathematics classrooms will also be provided.

Arming teachers to investigate!

This chapter has examined the nature of mathematical reasoning and the value of developing problem-solving and investigative approaches. Despite their inclusion and status in the national curriculum in England and Wales together with an ever-increasing supply of teaching sources and resources, the implementation of these approaches remains disappointing and limited. Teachers may feel convinced and committed. They may have easy access to a wealth of activities and materials. What they may need is the personal confidence and experience to plan successfully for these approaches in their mathematics curriculums. They may need guidance on *how* to teach rather than *what* to teach.

On reflection we recognize that we both arrived at our current understanding of how to teach through very similar experiences. Our journeys both began as learners when we tackled problem-solving and investigating. Experiencing the struggle and eventually the success of arriving at a solution or discovery firsthand had a huge impact on us both as learners and as teachers. It proved to be a powerful way of not just convincing us of the value of enquiry-based approaches but also in enabling us to begin to understand the distinct nature and purposes of both problem solving and investigations. Further we are convinced that our better understanding of *how* to teach has continued to evolve over many years of experience as teachers. So is it possible to provide a *shortcut* that enthuses and enables younger and possibly less experienced teachers to successfully plan for the development of mathematical reasoning in their classrooms? We propose that this could involve providing frameworks for teachers which reveal the nature and structure of the enquiry process. These frameworks could also scaffold teaching and learning. In our experience providing a straightforward structure for teachers can begin the process of evolving their own personal approach and philosophy to teaching. This structure need not become a straitjacket which inhibits and constrains teachers. Rather, it could provide the confidence to get started while being flexible enough to allow teachers the freedom to interpret and implement creatively in countless contexts.

In order to explain these frameworks it is necessary to consider the distinct nature of both problem-solving and investigative activities. Problem-solving activities are sometimes distinguished as being set in real, meaningful contexts and about real-life challenges, while investigations may involve 'context-free' and abstract ideas. We suggest that a more useful way of differentiating between them may be to consider their particular structure and processes the teacher can employ to scaffold pupils' learning. Table 3.2 presents pictures for problem-solving and investigative activities which may be helpful when beginning to consider how they could each be characterized.

Ways to problem solve and investigate

Table 3.2 Diagrams of problem-solving and investigative approaches

Diagram	Activity	Descriptors/Attributes
Broad (messy) start — Limited (neat) outcome/s — CLOSED	Problem solving *Squaring up to the problem* *Changing times*	• Broad (*messy*) start • Presents criteria, limits and constraints to be understood and conformed to, making it purposeful and demanding. • Necessitates prioritizing, interpreting and arranging information
Focused (neat) start — Multiple (messy) outcomes — OPEN ENDED	Investigating *Number strings* *Big questions:* *Best coffee?*	• Focused (*neat*) start • Can be quickly explained and understood, making it more accessible • Encourages asking questions with increasing independence of thought

A straightforward structure but not a straitjacket

Identifying descriptors for each of the types of activities begins to give *shape* to their distinctive nature. Perhaps more significantly this shape begins to reveal how these differences necessitate differences in how a teacher will need to plan to structure and scaffold teaching and learning. Despite their specific differences we believe that both types of activities have a particular *pulse* that can provide a reassuring rhythm that ensures the teacher and ultimately the pupils make progress.

When a teacher provides a pupil with a checklist of rules (such as RUCSAC or IDEAL) the teaching and inevitably the learning can be concerned with the application of a checklist of prescribed *procedures*. In contrast we suggest that being aware of a pulse and expressing this in terms of the *processes* rather than the *procedures* can be more useful. It can provide teachers with a 'user-friendly' and flexible framework that guides their teaching and drives pupils' learning within any problem-solving or investigative activity. The teacher and pupils could travel through each of the processes backwards and forwards and just one or multiple times regardless of the journey taking place over possibly shorter *built-in* or longer *bolt-on activities*.

When teaching responds to processes rather than procedures, pupils' learning is shifted from passively *following* the rules of others to actively *forming* relationships of their own.

50

The 3Es: enabling, engaging, evaluating

Our personal experiences of working with pupils, students and teachers have convinced us that expressing that *pulse* as three particular processes: *enabling, engaging and evaluating* can encourage greater confidence, commitment and creativity.

Enabling

Despite their distinct and different nature, both problem-solving and investigative activities present teachers with the same initial challenge to *enable* pupils to *make a start*: to be able to purposefully participate. How the teacher enables pupils will be different and determined by the type of activity to be introduced. A problem-solving activity will typically present a broad (*messy*) start, which pupils may find complex, confusing and even overwhelmingly challenging. So it is the teacher's responsibility/task to creatively plan to clarify and communicate the particular criteria, limits and constraints that need to be understood and conformed to within the problem. Embedded in the teacher's presentation of the challenge should be opportunities that allow learners to interpret, prioritize, sort, arrange and organize information. For example, try encouraging collaboration and discussion through shared resources and the requirement for an agreed shared solution (see Chapter 5 in this text). Further, the teacher must ensure that the context and method of presenting the activity has meaning, purpose and significance to the pupils so that the problem is worth solving. For example, the use of time provides a familiar context that enables pupils to draw on their own knowledge to more readily understand the demands and begin to consider the implications of changes posed in the problem (see Chapter 7 in this text).

An investigative activity will, in contrast, pose a more focused (*neat*) start, which provides all pupils with a common single line of inquiry, which can be explored and extended. For example, posing 'What is the best coffee?' provides a brief and direct question that pupils can readily understand and begin to explore according to their own experiences, interests and ideas. The design of this initial *hook* is crucial. It must be at a level which is accessible to the majority and ideally all learners while being demanding and intriguing enough for multiple lines of inquiry to be pursued at different levels and depths. For example, simply asking pupils to think of any two consecutive numbers and add them provides a speedy and uncomplicated means of enabling them to participate in the investigative process (see Chapter 4 in this text). Initially the playful generation of series of sums and calculation of answers provides opportunities for pupils to identify relatively obvious patterns and relationships. The intention is that this ready access encourages confidence and interest that stimulates the pupils to consider other related lines of inquiry.

Engaging

A well-designed and clearly presented hook initiates pupils' engagement in the problem-solving or investigative process and begins to shift the emphasis away from the teacher's question. This movement from the teacher's questions towards the pupils' own questions necessitates changes in the teacher's role as an initiator and presenter. As pupils evolve and pursue different lines to inquiry the teacher strives to facilitate and support. Their teaching focus shifts from enthusing and *enabling* to encouraging and *engaging*. In order to solve a problem or explore a line of inquiry pupils need to select and employ a range of strategies. For pupils to make progress teachers need to support them to make increasingly informed decisions about their choices from a range of strategies and to use these strategies with increasing efficiency. This range of strategies should continue to expand and could include trial and improvement methods, finding all possibilities, identifying patterns and trends, simplifying and relating to similar situations, eliminating and deriving additional information, drawing tables and diagrams and working backwards.

Evaluating

The playful and persistent application of strategies is crucial to pupils' purposeful engagement in the enquiry process. Although the process may be common to both problem-solving and investigative activities the purposes for this engagement will be different. This inevitably impacts the role of the teacher, as they re-focus pupils' learning from the process of *engaging* to the process of *evaluating*. In problem solving their engagement allows pupils to move towards a narrowing set of solutions. So the process of *evaluating* will involve pupils explaining their possible solution(s) to a particular problem. Here the teacher's role is to challenge pupils to support the appropriateness and quality of the solution by also justifying and being convincing about the efficiency of their approach. In contrast, while pupils are investigating, their engagement inspires them to explore a widening number of discoveries and inventions. The process of *evaluating* involves pupils in explaining their discoveries and new ideas. Here the teacher is challenging the pupils to justify and prove the validity of new discoveries. As a consequence the construction and reconstruction of conceptual understanding causes an invention of new ways of thinking.

Table 3.3 extends Table 3.2 to summarize the 3Es in relation to problem-solving and investigative activities.

52

Ways to problem solve and investigate

Table 3.3 Adding 3 Es to the table

Diagram	Activity	Processes
(inverted triangle diagram: Enabling, Engaging, Evaluating)	**Problem Solving**	**Enabling** pupils to understand and interpret the requirements of the *messy* problem and become motivated to find a *neat* solution
	Squaring up to the problem	**Engaging** pupils in the application of strategies for playfully and systematically pursuing lines of inquiry *(e.g. trial and improvement, finding all possibilities, identifying patterns and trends, simplifying and relating to similar situations, eliminating and deriving additional information, drawing tables and diagrams, working backwards etc.)*
	Changing times	**Evaluating** learning, with emphasis on: (i) justifying and being convincing about the efficiency of approach (ii) appropriateness and quality of solution for the problem.
(triangle diagram: Enabling, Engaging, Evaluating)	**Investigating**	**Enabling** pupils to move away from a *neat* starting point and be inspired to purse messy lines of inquiry with increasing independence **Engaging** pupils in the application of strategies for playfully and systematically pursuing lines of inquiry *(e.g. trial and improvement, finding all possibilities, identifying patterns and trends simplifying and relating to similar situations, eliminating and deriving additional information, drawing tables and diagrams, working backwards etc.)*
	Number strings	**Evaluating** learning, with emphasis on:
	Big questions	(i) justifying and explaining the validity of new ideas
	Best coffee?	(ii) the construction and reconstruction of conceptual understanding (mental models) and invention of new ways of thinking.

Ways to problem solve and investigate

Explaining, predicting, diagnosing

Students undertaking the Post Graduate Certificate in Education (PGCE) part-time route at a London university participated in a research activity in which they taught the same lesson to pupils from Year Three to Year Six in a west London Primary school in April 2015. The lesson was 'Number Strings' (see Chapter 4 this text), and the students used the processes Enabling, Engaging and Evaluating within the Mode Typology Framework *to structure their planning*. While all PGCE students in the group ($n = 22$) taught the lesson, 11 participated in the research aspect of the activity thereby providing informed consent following ethical guidelines (BERA, 2011) for their responses to a survey subsequent to the activity to be used here. We were interested in their reflections on the usefulness of the key questions, which were provided to them on coloured palm cards to use while interacting with the Primary school pupils who were doing the investigation. Figure 3.1 shows the cyclical approach that we anticipated the Primary pupils would undergo as they sought solutions to their increasingly sophisticated investigations into number strings.

What was clear from the responses provided by the participating PGCE students was that the questions provided were used throughout and were effective in guiding them to prompt the children both to think more deeply about what they were doing and to articulate their findings as they progressed. The questions for each function were started with a different question word: Explaining used *how*, Predicting used *what* and, Diagnosing used *why*. Another function, Communicating, was also included, and its question word was *could*. One participating PGCE student suggested, "The questions were fairly self-explanatory. I would have liked to think that I would have used them anyway", while another "found that the cards really elevated the idea of questioning in my mind; it gave a focus to my interactions with children". Their open-ended responses and numerical data about the actual questions used have been useful in guiding us as to the efficacy of the typology to support thinking and learning.

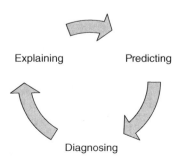

Figure 3.1 Explaining, Predicting, Diagnosing functions of the Mental Model Mode

Coloured question cards were provided to the PGCE students to enable them to prompt children and are shown in Figure 3.2. There were two cards for each of the Explaining (blue) and Predicting (red) functions while the Diagnosing (green) and Communicating (purple) functions had one card each. The Communicating function aspect was less of a focus and was included to guide the PGCE students through a closing activity in which the Primary pupils would be prompted to reflect on their actions and thoughts to see if they could convince them of what they had learned. Some feedback was given by those participating in the research on the use of the typology about Communicating, and it will be addressed in a later chapter (see Chapter 8).

Of the 11 PGCE students who participated in the research, all of them used the first of the Explaining prompts, "How can you explain what you are noticing?" We also suggested before the lessons that the PGCE students might find that using a stem

Blue Cards: Explaining

How can you explain what you are noticing?

100 square? Sequence?

How can you explain your findings?

Words? Resources? Pictures? Algebra?

Red Cards: Predicting

What do you think will be the result if you ...? Investigate longer sums? Investigate how to find even answers?

What can you use this information to do next...? Find another answer? Take another step? Have you considered every possibility?

Green Card: Diagnosing

Why didn't it work? Why might you try something else? Why did it work?

Purple Card: Communicating

Could you convince someone about what you ...? Found out? Know? Think? Have learned? Understand? Believe?

Summary

Explaining (How) Predicting (What)

Diagnosing (Why) Communicating (Could)

Figure 3.2 Mode Typology prompt cards used with number strings activity, 2015

question such as "How can you explain . . ." might allow instead of enable them to be more fluent with the prompt because they would be using it idiosyncratically, adapting the prompt to suit the situation and child rather than repeating a standard question. This approach was useful, with one student responding, "I used this sentence stem and adapted it with language I was more comfortable with such as *How can you explain the relationship between the algebraic formulae?*" While one PGCE student found the prompts "effective to scaffold children of lesser ability", another found them "most effective as a challenge to high-ability children" which indicates that the prompts do not have to be altered significantly to suit the capability or confidence of any child in any of the classes in which such an activity is being done.

The feedback on the Explaining function was quite predictable, because it is the most common action that teachers will ask pupils to do in their classrooms regardless of sector or subject. However, the use of prediction, while promoted by the mathematics curriculum (DfE, 2013), is not always included in activities, and we have rarely seen Diagnosing addressed in any mathematics lessons we have viewed as tutors. The most commonly used Diagnosing question was "Why did it work?" and this would indicate that the Primary pupils were able to explain a process they used that was successful, relying on knowledge of cause and effect that Johnson-Laird (2008) suggested was preferred by pupils because they would rather go beyond a minimal explanation when looking for the most probable answer. But one of the PGCE students found that she used more specific questions in the Diagnosing stage because "the more open-ended questions led to more blank stares". This is not a situation you would like to be in as either a teacher or a student, but experienced teachers would agree that it does happen and does require you to rethink quickly in order to lead children forward with their thinking. While the Diagnosing questions helped pupils to "clarify where they went wrong", as one PGCE student noted, many children could not explain why. At this point, when faced with a pupil who is stalled in their thinking, it is advisable to return to the Explaining prompts to establish what they do know as safe ground for recommencing the investigative journey.

The use of multiple unstructured resources also enabled the Primary pupils to enter the problem space of the number strings activity at this time with greater confidence. When one of the PGCE students was posing an Explaining prompt, she found that "resources were critical in helping the children spot the patterns in the first place and articulate what they noticed". The inclusion of prompts on the Explaining cards in Figure 3.2 for questions about using the *100 square* or to find a *sequence* enabled the PGCE students to make decisions as to what level of support or guidance was necessary for the pupils they were working with. Such prompts would not necessarily be included for the variety of problem-solving activities that pupils would be exposed to in their Primary school classes. Anghileri (1995, p. 7) linked resources to "active participation in problem solving through practical tasks, pattern seeking and sharing understanding", and such use of resources to show what the pupils understood was clear in this activity. The provision of an explicit link to those resources on the prompt cards ensured that the PGCE students, who are still learning the craft of teaching, would not forget to encourage the pupils they were teaching to make use of the resources not only in their active construction of knowledge but also in their attempts to explain, predict and diagnose. So Drews (2007) recommends quite rightly that teachers need to be very clear about why they are providing the resources they are for certain activities and that they should also have an understanding of the relationship between the task itself and any visual imagery that might be attributed to it. Here the resources were also linked very explicitly to the functions of the Mode, thereby providing further evidence of the Mode's efficacy to support problem-solving and investigational activity.

Moving forward . . .

The following four chapters present ideas on the use of the framework and *our* approach to developing mathematical reasoning. These are considered with the intention to *enable* pupils to *engage* in rich activities that sharpen their appetites for learning in an environment that celebrates risk taking and provides time and opportunities to *evaluate* their creative thinking.

References

Anderson, L. W., & Krathwohl, D. R. (2001). *A taxonomy for learning, teaching, and assessing: A revision of Bloom's taxonomy of educational objectives.* London, UK: Longman.

Anghileri, J. (Ed.). (1995). *Children's mathematical thinking in the primary years: Perspectives on children's learning.* London, UK: Cassell.

Arnot, C. (2005). Interview with Professor Sir Christopher Zeeman. *Warwick The Magazine,* Spring(6), 20–21.

Askew, M. (2012). *Transforming primary mathematics.* Oxon, UK: Routledge.

Barmby, P., Bolden, D., & Thompson, L. (2014). *Understanding and enriching problem solving in primary mathematics.* Northwich, UK: Critical Publishing Ltd.

British Educational Research Association (BERA). (2011). *Ethic*al guidelines for educational research. London, UK: BERA. [Online] Available at: https://www.bera.ac.uk/wp-content/uploads/2014/02/BERA-Ethical-Guidelines-2011.pdf?noredirect=1

Bloom, B. S. (Ed.). (1956). *Taxonomy of educational objectives, the classification of educational goals – handbook I: Cognitive domain.* New York, NY: McKay.

Burton, L. (1986). *Thinking things through*. Oxford: Blackwell.

Department for Education (2013). *The national curriculum for England and Wales*. London, UK: DfE.

Drews, D. (2007). Do resources matter in primary mathematics teaching and learning? In D. Drews & A. Hansen (Eds.), *Using resources to support mathematical thinking: Primary and early years* (pp. 19–31). Exeter, UK: Learning Matters Ltd.

Edwards-Leis, C. E. (2013). Knowing where the shoe pinches: Using the Mental Model Mode to understand how primary pupils an design intelligently. In *Technology education for the future: A play on sustainability, PATT27 Conference* (pp. 141–148). Christchurch, NZ: University of Waikato.

Fairclough, R. (2011). Developing problem-solving skills in mathematics. In V. Koshy & J. Murray (Eds.), *Unlocking mathematics teaching* (pp. 84–109). Oxon, UK: Routledge.

Haylock, D. (2010). *Mathematics explained for primary teachers* (4th ed.). London, UK: SAGE Publications Ltd.

Johnson-Laird, P. N. (2008). *How we reason*. Oxford, UK: Oxford University Press.

Jonassen, D. H. (2011). *Learning to solve problems: A handbook for designing problem-solving learning environments*. New York, NY: Routledge.

Nickerson, R. S. (1994). The teaching of thinking and problem solving. In R. J. Sternberg (Ed.), *Thinking and problem solving* (pp. 409–449). London, UK: Academic Press.

Ofsted (2012). *Mathematics: Made to measure*, UK, No. 110159. [Online] Available at: https://www.gov.uk/government/publications/mathematics-made-to-measure

Orton, A., & Frobisher, L. (1999). *Insights into teaching mathematics*. London, UK: Cassell.

Polya, G. (1957). *How to solve it* (2nd ed.). Princeton, NJ: Princeton University Press.

Pretz, J. E., Naples, A. J., & Sternberg, R. J. (2003). Recognizing, defining, and representing problems. In J. E. Davidson & R. J. Sternberg (Eds.), *The psychology of problem solving* (pp. 3–30). Cambridge: Cambridge University Press.

Riley, M. S., Greeno, J. G., & Heller, J. I. (1983). Development of children's problem solving ability in arithmetic. In H. P. Ginsburg (Ed.), *The development of mathematical thinking*. New York, NY: Academic Press.

Rumelhart, D. E., & Ortony, A. (1977). The representation of knowledge in memory. In R. C. Anderson, R. J. Spire, & W. E. Montague (Eds.), *Schooling and the acquisition of knowledge* (pp. 99–135). Hillsdale, NJ: Lawrence Erlbaum.

Vosniadou, S. (2002). Mental models in conceptual development. In L. Magnani & N. Nersessian (Eds.), *Model-based reasoning: Science, technology, values.* New York, NY: Kluwer Academic Press.

Williams, P. (2008). *Independent review of mathematics teaching in early years settings and primary schools.* Final Report. London, UK: Department for Children, Schools and Families.

Websites

NCETM, National centre for excellence in the teaching of mathematics, Cert No. 2702 ISO 9001, www.ncetm.org.uk

NRICH, University of Cambridge (1997–2016) as part of the Millennium Mathematics Project, http://nrich.maths.org/frontpage

4 | **Number strings**

Relational mathematics and identity

When Williams (2008) published his findings in the *Independent Review of Mathematics Teaching in Early Years Settings and Primary Schools* an unequivocal message was delivered to those who are passionate about providing the best mathematical learning environment for our young people. His identification of the critical prerequisite of Primary teachers to be both confident and competent in teaching mathematics (Williams, 2008) confirmed the evidence in the Cockcroft Report (1982), which foregrounds the importance of children being exposed to as wide as possible a variety of mathematical experiences and to have had the opportunity to discuss mathematics with their teacher and their peers. Teachers who lack competence and confidence are more inclined to limit the experiences, particularly in problem solving and investigations that the children encounter due, in the main, to their own anxiety of being exposed as impotent during the process. Much of the report (Cockcroft, 1982) talks about *being numerate*, particularly in the sense of being able to participate in the world of work and using mental arithmetic in a variety of work contexts. In particular employers at the time the report was compiled found that newly hired teenagers who demonstrated little competence in arithmetic when employed soon gained competency once they learned why it was necessary to carry out specific calculations. The importance of context remains unambiguous and imposes on teachers from all sectors the need to engage learners in real enquiries and activities for which mathematics has a real purpose, which we propose can be more authentically created in a rich and challenging mathematical learning environment.

An important aspect of being a competent and confident teacher of mathematics at Primary school is identifying as someone who can 'do' mathematics. Askew, Brown, Rhodes, Wiliam and Johnson (1997) recognized that to be an effective teacher of numeracy (rather than mathematics in general) the teacher had to have knowledge of the conceptual connections between the areas in the curriculum. Later Askew (2012) would refer to this phenomenon as teachers having a 'connectionist orientation' in which they have a consistent and coherent set of beliefs about how best to teach mathematics that took into account how children learn. He suggested that having such an orientation encompassed two characteristics: the ability to make connections within mathematics (its difference aspects and representations) and the ability to make connections with children's methods of thinking and processing.

A teacher's orientation toward mathematics, while having particular characteristics and subsequent influences on what happens in the mathematics activities in and outside of the classroom (Askew, 2012), is clearly linked to the perception of competence, or mental model of mathematical capability, that the individual holds. We have encountered competent all-round learners on the Post Graduate Certificate in Education (PGCE) courses we teach who may have received a First in their undergraduate degree in history or literature but who have a quasi-functional mental model of mathematics capability. We say 'quasi-functional' because on the face of it the student teachers are numerate and able to function as successful humans in society. However, when probed by course tutors during initial workshops in Primary mathematics, their functionality is exposed as what Richard Skemp (1976/2006) would term 'instrumental'. Instrumental understanding of mathematics, as used by Skemp in both his seminal work in 1976 and republished in 2006, means that the individual is able to execute or carry out mathematical procedures, rules and operations. We would probably call this being numerate or having a functional mental model of mathematics. However, when tutors start to probe student teachers during mathematics courses it soon becomes apparent that a fair proportion of them do not have the 'relational understanding' of mathematics that Skemp proposed as being "knowing what to do and *why*" (Skemp, 2006, p. 89, our italics). If a teacher themselves only has an instrumental understanding of mathematics then it is unlikely that they will be able to develop in their learners such an important cognitive awareness.

Skemp (1976/2006) talks about mismatches between teachers and learners of their 'orientation' towards either type of learning as causing a serious problem particularly if the mismatch occurs between a learner who seeks to understand relationally and a teacher who teaches instrumentally. Like Skemp (1976/2006) tutors on our PGCE mathematics course were aware of there being a potential for two different subjects to be taught due to the expectations of the student teachers in each group: those with established relational understanding were comfortable probing cognitive development and schematic understanding of concepts, while those with instrumental understanding wanted to 'learn the process or method'. Many student teachers themselves were bemused at the difference in approach they were experiencing in a class in which instruction was designed to enable them to become teachers of mathematics: we'll all be teaching the same curriculum, so why do we see it as a different process?

Both instrumental and relational understanding of mathematics are useful for learners (Skemp, 1976/2006), and while instrumental approaches provide immediate reward for effort, relational understanding is more portable and enables the learner to continue to develop more functional mental models of mathematics throughout their life because a strong network of understandings has been developed (Edwards-Leis, 2010). Therefore, developing a relational understanding of mathematics is the focus for this chapter because we believe that teachers who have a 'quasi-functional' mental model of mathematics are less likely to teach relational understanding of mathematics and may, in reality, limit the exposure that learners have to the problem-solving and investigative aspects of the subject that will set them up as learners for life. In essence, part of the work that we do with student teachers is encourage them to construct their identity as a competent and confident teacher of mathematics. Pratt's (2012) work on constructing identity helps to inform our approaches in our mathematics workshops. He talks about how an individual will construct their identity by both acting (working) and reacting (customizing) with others in a social environment, which instantiates a relational base for identity formation (Pratt, 2012, p. 26). This social identity approach is very useful when working with differences in groups such as those evident in a Primary mathematics workshop group. It enables differences to be exposed through mental models of mathematics which can be discussed, compared, analyzed and evaluated for functionality particularly in a teaching/learning situation. We found that the task outlined in this chapter created the context for individuals to reflect, share and challenge their existing identity as a learner of mathematics. The results were startling, because for the first time in some student teachers' lives they had developed a relational understanding of algebra and were less fearful of teaching mathematics to the children who would be in their charge.

The re-emergence of algebra

We often use video to demonstrate key ideas when conducting workshops with student teachers of Primary mathematics. One such video was *Twice Five Plus the Wings of a Bird* (BBC Television, 1986), in which a variety of presenters interviewed average working people to discover their attitudes towards mathematics. One such segment looked at scaffolders using Pythagoras's theory without any idea of its source: it's just a, b, c, several commented. Repetitive use and increased familiarity contribute to the mental model that such calculations cease to be thought of as mathematics and instead becomes part of the job or life. Cockcroft (1982, p. 19) earlier commented that such individuals saw this use as ". . . not mathematics, it's common sense" which also indicates an 'at-homeness' with a particular *piece* of mathematics.

The Cockcroft Report (Cockcroft, 1982, p. 20) also mentions mental calculations in both Primary and Secondary settings and how mental approaches to mathematics are allowed to atrophy due to lack of practice in the classroom. A reliance on pen and paper recording providing 'evidence' of work seems to be creeping into the current lexicon of mathematical classroom practice and overrides a teacher's use of mental processes because a teacher is unable to *prove* that certain work has been covered adequately unless some well-marked artifact is provided. Of particular interest for this chapter are Cockcroft's (1982) findings, in which there was little *explicit* use of algebra in the workplace. Formulae *were* used, but often words replaced the single letters (*a, b, x, y*) most commonly found in classroom-based formulae. Technicians, craftspeople and clerical workers tended to use some formulae, but most managed such exercises by replacing the words with figures and relied on calculators to complete the task (Cockcroft, 1982). We have seen a re-emergence of explicit algebra in Primary settings in England and Wales since the current mathematics curriculum was released (DfE, 2013), and such unambiguous inclusion has raised the anxiety levels of many student teachers entering the profession with little relational understanding of this fundamental branch of mathematics.

Algebra in the Primary setting (in certain parts of the world)

Algebra emerges formally in the Primary curriculum in mathematics in England and Wales (DfE, 2013) in Year Six when learners are age 10 to 11 years. We would argue that algebra enters mathematics in classrooms informally much earlier than this. The term 'algebraically' does emerge in the Year Four Measurement Notes and Guidance for Non-Statutory section stating "Perimeter can be expressed algebraically as $2(a + b)$ where a and b are the dimensions in the same unit" (DfE, 2013, p. 28). However, it is not until the Year Six level that we see algebra as a statutory requirement with its own strand.

The statutory requirements for algebra state that learners "should be taught to:

- Use simple formulae;
- Generate and describe linear number sequences;
- Express missing number problems algebraically;
- Find pairs of numbers that satisfy an equation with two unknowns;
- Enumerate possibilities of combinations of two variables" (DfE, 2013, p. 42).

The non-statutory notes and guidance offer more ideas for incorporation into the algebraic learning environment by suggesting learners:

". . . should be introduced to the use of symbols and letters to represent variables and unknowns in mathematical situations that they already understand, such as:

- Missing numbers, lengths, coordinates and angles;
- Formulae in mathematics and science;
- Equivalent expressions (for example, $a + b = b + a$);
- Generalizations of number patterns;
- Number puzzles (for example, what two numbers can add up to) (DfE, 2013, p. 43).

Other mention of 'algebra' or 'algebraically' in the Year Six curriculum guidance occurs where there are possible relationships between measures or shapes and their parts such as the relationship between angles and lengths in "$d = 2 \times r$" (DfE, 2013, p. 44) and the algebraic expression of polygons as coordinates "for example, translating vertex (a,b) to $(a - 2, b + 3)$" (DfE, 2013, p. 45). It would seem that such a significant area of mathematics and one that has the potential in later years of schooling to contribute to so much anxiety for so many individuals enters the statutory requirements with little fanfare. It almost slips in under the radar while simultaneously taking on demonic characteristics and form. Well, that may be an exaggeration, but we have seen grown people tremble when faced with an assignment that requires them to explore algebra in no less than 12 A4 pages! Debbie, as an experienced teacher of mathematics, knew that there was only one way to engage student teachers in a mathematics challenge that would both provide authentic Eureka moments of joyous learning and also ensure that they developed an instrumental understanding of and approach to the teaching of mathematics: number strings provides the building blocks that support, provoke and challenge learners to develop a rich and robust algebraic understanding, and it does so by asking them to add two numbers together and see what happens.

Number strings

Number strings is an investigation with a focused or neat start that can be quickly explained and understood to learners of all ages or abilities. This simplistic entry point makes it more accessible for a wide range of children: we took the activity to a local Primary school and, with the support of 22 student teachers, shared it successfully with learners aged from 7 to 11 years. The activity encourages asking questions (both children and teachers!) with the aim that children will have increased independence of thought as they progress through the investigation. It is an individual activity, although children can choose to work in pairs at different points throughout the investigation. The longed-for "Ah-ha" moments, though, will often come when children have the opportunity, and courage, to work independently. While the activity is focused at the start, there is no limit as to where the children can take the investigation. Therefore, it is 'messy' at the end, with multiple outcomes that are only limited by time, resources and perhaps the tenacity of the individual. We have seen student teachers recalibrate their identity as mathematicians and as teachers of mathematics after being engaged with this activity.

The activity formed an integral component of our assessment strategy with student teachers for many years at the university where we work. The outline of this assessment task is presented in Appendix 1 including the assessment focus on the quality of the student teacher's informed analytical or creative insights into the identification of personal mathematical development. Such development was in relation to mathematical understanding, thinking skills, attitudes towards and appreciation of mathematics. We asked that student teachers 'create headlines' and 'summarize their learning process through identification of significant factors that influenced, supported and enabled them to extend their understanding, analytical skills and appreciation of mathematics'. Lesh and Clarke (2000, p. 143) commented that such approaches are antithetical to usual assessments which "seldom include descriptions, explanations, or justifications in which they must reveal and test explicitly how they interpret problem solving situations". Indeed, Lesh and Clarke (2000, p. 143) felt that most kinds of assessment focus on quantification and "rarely go beyond the simple count and measures". We understood that in order to develop teachers who were willing to engage their pupils in problem solving and investigations that were relational and therefore meaningful, we would need to challenge the existing quasi-functional mental models of mathematics that student teachers were presenting when they entered university. So, what did we require student teachers and the children at the local Primary school to do?

The task: enabling

Children will start at a *neat* starting point which requires them to add consecutive numbers to see what happens. As they progress in their activity they will usually be inspired to pursue increasingly messy lines of inquiry but with greater independence at various plateau points. Plateaus are inevitable because children will reach points at which they believe they understand exactly what is happening and be able to predict what will happen next. At this point, careful prompting and questioning should make the plateau somewhat unstable, thereby challenging the learner to review their strategy and move on to a different course of investigation.

Number strings

Various materials are necessary for the starting point of the task, and these should be available for all learners in abundance. Materials should include:

- Hundred squares
- Multi-link cubes of various colours
- Paper for recording

The first instruction is for learners to add consecutive numbers and record what happens on their hundred square.

1	2	3	4	5	6	7	8	9	10
11	12	13	14	15	16	17	18	19	20
21	22	23	24	25	26	27	28	29	30
31	32	33	34	35	36	37	38	39	40
41	42	43	44	45	46	47	48	49	50
51	52	53	54	55	56	57	58	59	60
61	62	63	64	65	66	67	68	69	70
71	72	73	74	75	76	77	78	79	80
81	82	83	84	85	86	87	88	89	90
91	92	93	94	95	96	97	98	99	100

1 + 2 = 3
2 + 3 = 5
3 + 4 = 7
4 + 5 = 9
5 + 6 = 11
6 + 7 = 13
7 + 8 = 15
47 + 48 = 95
48 + 49 = 97

Learners will start to see that their addition of consecutive numbers results in a pattern forming on the hundred square, which will be evident by the colouring of the odd numbers on the square. You would encourage the learners to show this phenomena using multi-link blocks as well. In the first instance encourage the use of colour to represent different integers – here numbers one to four are represented by different shades of greyscale.

1 + 2 = 3

2 + 3 = 5

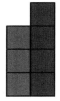

3 + 4 = 7

The results replicate what the learners would have recorded on their paper and on the 100 squares. It is important to allow learners to continue this process until they are confident that they can see the pattern of arriving at an odd number when adding consecutive numbers. They should be able to articulate:

Number strings

When I add two consecutive numbers the answer is always an odd number.

To test this prediction, ask learners to choose any two consecutive numbers. What will delight many is the opportunity to choose very large or 'difficult' numbers to add. Evaluating the answer as being an odd number will reinforce the children's understanding of oddness by encouraging them to explain their answer and prove that it is odd. Once children are comfortable with this knowledge challenge them to see if they can develop a rule for adding the entire set of consecutive numbers. Some children may arrive at the formula $2n + 1$ by themselves, but if they struggle, the use of the Mode Typology prompts will enable children to progress. For example, asking the question What do you think you will find if you change the colour of your blocks like this? You would then demonstrate for the entire group or class the following:

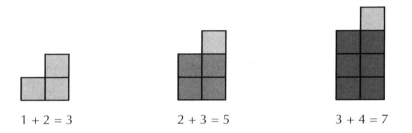

1 + 2 = 3   2 + 3 = 5   3 + 4 = 7

This visual display would be held up for all of the children to see, and you would wait for the children to respond with what they have observed. If the responses are slow to arrive, you can prompt them to compare the original arrays with the new ones by using an Explaining prompt from the Mode Typology: How can you explain what you notice when you compare the different arrays for adding 2 + 3 = 5?

What you are aiming to receive in explanation is that 5 is the result of doubling 2 and then adding 1. In other words, we should be able to predict the answer to the addition of two consecutive numbers by doubling the first of the numbers and adding one. The universal formula to test will be, where n equals the first number added:

$$2n + 1$$

Again, the universality of the formula to work correctly for all possible numbers will provide the opportunity for children to use any numbers they wish to test the formula as long as the ones selected are whole numbers. You may wish to explore the effect if using fractional numbers, but the formula is designed for whole numbers. Once all learners are comfortable with this first plateau, you are ready to really engage them in the investigation.

Engaging

Once the learners have entered the investigations and been enabled to start their exploration, the engaging stage will give them the opportunity to apply strategies playfully and systematically to pursue different lines of enquiry. In this activity the strategies to use include:

- finding all possibilities;
- identifying patterns and trends;
- simplifying and relating to similar situations;
- eliminating and deriving additional information; and,
- drawing tables and diagrams to illustrate findings.

The time you give to the students to explore the different options will be dependent on the space you can provide in your timetable. There will, of course, be differences in how successful problem solvers go about investigating the possibilities for this activity compared to those who are less confident. Xin, Wiles and Lin (2008) found that those who are more successful look beyond the surface features of any investigation in order to analyze the underlying structure of the problem. This work confirmed earlier work by Newton (1996), who believed that novice problem solvers lacked the repertoire of conceptual, procedural and declarative or propositional knowledge necessary to respond to problem situations with broad tactical know-how. They tended to deal with the surface characteristics because the mental models they needed for problem solving were only weakly linked if connected at all. Teachers, too, can have novice mental models of problem solving and investigating, and if they are not provided with the support to guide learners through such challenges, then the potential for children to leave Primary school with insufficient problem-solving mental models is increased. Entering this engaging stage can be guided by the teacher with another neat starting point in order to focus children on the many possibilities for investigation.

From random to systematic: a balance between prescription and ad-hoc!

We value the opportunity that student teachers have to respond randomly to the number strings or consecutive sums activity. However, it is important to provide guidance to children on how they can benefit from the randomness of open exploration to the scaffolding of a systematic approach. We would suggest following the prompts that follow to commence this stage of the investigation either as a mini-plenary session

Number strings

following the enabling stage from earlier or as a new, discrete follow-on lesson at another time.

Provide children with abundant squares of paper. The size doesn't really matter, nor does the quality. What you are aiming for is that groups of children can work at tables, with another whole-class collection being demonstrated at the front of the class. The teacher would prompt:

What happens when you add three consecutive numbers? Write your string of numbers and the answer on a piece of paper. If you have time, do another one.

What will generally happen, if given sufficient time, children will come up with a myriad of answers as shown here.

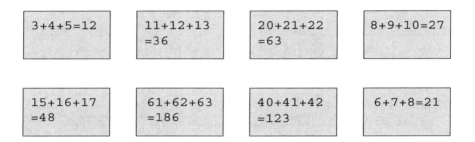

The teacher should then ask the children in their groups to put all of the cards in order of the answer size. She may choose to demonstrate this process at the front with a few selected cards. With the cards shown, the result of ordering will be:

| 12 | 21 | 27 | 36 | 48 | 63 | 123 | 186 |

The next direction would be to ask the children whether there are any results missing between these answers. If we take answers between 12 and 21 as an example, children should respond that the following are missing:

$$4 + 5 + 6 = 15$$
$$5 + 6 + 7 = 18$$

When put these results are placed into the sequence, it would now read:

12, 15, 18, 21

A Mode Typology prompt would follow if children cannot detect the pattern. How can you explain our findings? This question would enable the explanation function to be enacted but should be followed by a prediction prompt, What can you use this information to do next? Or What would you do to find the next answer?

Prompting the learners to also use their 100 square to record all of the possible answers up to 100 will show the pattern:

1	2	3	4	5	6	7	8	9	10
11	12	13	14	15	16	17	18	19	20
21	22	23	24	25	26	27	28	29	30
31	32	33	34	35	36	37	38	39	40
41	42	43	44	45	46	47	48	49	50
51	52	53	54	55	56	57	58	59	60
61	62	63	64	65	66	67	68	69	70
71	72	73	74	75	76	77	78	79	80
81	82	83	84	85	86	87	88	89	90
91	92	93	94	95	96	97	98	99	100

If children were able to demonstrate the pattern by using multi-link cubes they would show an emerging sequence as shown here:

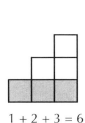 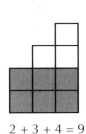 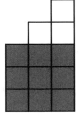

1 + 2 + 3 = 6   2 + 3 + 4 = 9   3 + 4 + 5 = 12

What they would be seeing is that if the first number in the sequence (e.g. 1) is multiplied by three (being the number of digits added) followed by adding 3 (the number of digits added) a formula can be created:

$$3n + 3$$

It is then possible to use a Mode Typology prompt to enact the diagnostic function of thinking to see if the formula works for all possibilities.

$$3n + 3 =$$
$$3 \times 1 + 3 = 6$$
$$3 \times 2 + 3 = 9$$
$$3 \times 3 + 3 = 12$$

Once again, children will try out various combinations of digits to test the formula for as many number strings as possible. Using calculators for very large numbers also adds a useful challenge to the process and will capture the imagination of many children who may find large numbers quite daunting.

Once this process of taking random answers to develop a systematic approach is used with children they will feel more comfortable with brainstorming an idea because the teacher has provided a scaffold that will help them bring ideas together so that they make some meaning. At this point you would encourage children to find all possibilities, which may include some of the following:

- adding 4 to 10 consecutive numbers
- adding consecutive odd numbers
- adding consecutive even numbers

At each point you would be probing learners with appropriate prompts from the Mode Typology depending on their level of engagement and success. Explaining prompts will guide learners to use pictures, diagrams or formulae to express what they are finding. Predicting prompts will encourage them to investigate longer sums, find another answer or consider every possibility. The diagnostic function is very important if children are stalled because it prompts them to investigate why some strategy did or did not work. At the end of the session, which will be determined by how you, as a teacher, assess the engagement of the children and the success they are experiencing, it is important to have a plenary session in which ideas are shared and solutions evaluated.

Evaluating the activity

Evaluating what has been learned to establish its significance should never be shortened or removed from your lesson environment. It is the most important aspect of the learning that takes place, because it is the time when learners have the opportunity to make strong connection of ideas: it's a time of reflection, sharing, listening, absorbing and remembering. Askew (2012) agrees and suggests that a 10-minute plenary tacked on to the end of a lesson cannot resolve any misconceptions a child might have. We would suggest that, in this instance, the plenary could take a whole afternoon because it's not just about arriving at an understanding of an algebraic formula. We believe that you should emphasize justifying and explaining the validity of these new ideas with the class, which will enable all learners to construct and reconstruct their conceptual understanding or mental models of algebra, which will incorporate new ways of thinking, showing, testing and communicating.

Like the PGCE students who found so many Ah-ha moments when they undertook their 12-A4 page investigation of consecutive sums as part of their assessment, your students will value the opportunity to share what they have found and explore new possibilities. Apart from meeting the statutory requirements and non-statutory guidance embedded in the national curriculum of England and Wales (DfE, 2013) you would have demonstrated to the learners that there are many ways to *play* with numbers that allow them to act like explorers, as Zeeman would encourage, so as to discover new ways of thinking and communicating with numbers. Askew (2012) encourages teachers to take time with creative investigations because the incubation time is so necessary for true learning and understanding. We believe that through number strings children will come to know numbers better rather than just being able to reach an end result that has been predetermined by someone else. At the end of the number strings journey, the children would have 'done' mathematics and be well on their way to developing more algebraic knowledge.

References

Askew, M. (2012). *Transforming primary mathematics*. Oxon, UK: Routledge.

Askew, M., Brown, M., Rhodes, V., Wiliam, D., & Johnson, D. (1997). *Effective teachers of numeracy: Report of a study carried out for the Teacher Training Agency*. London, UK: King's College, University of London.

BBC Television. (1986). *Twice Five Plus the Wings of a Bird*. Horizon, Series. [Online] Available at: http://bufvc.ac.uk/dvdfind/index.php/title/22263 (Accessed 25 Apr 2018).

Cockcroft, W. H. (1982). *The Cockcroft report: Mathematics counts*. Report of the Committee of Inquiry into the teaching of Mathematics in Schools. London, UK: Her Majesty's Stationery Office.

Department for Education. (2013). *The national curriculum for England and Wales* London, UK: DfE.

Edwards-Leis, C.E. (2010). *Mental models of teaching, learning, and assessment A longitudinal study*. PhD thesis, James Cook University. [Online] Available at: eprints.jcu.edu.au/15182/1/01Thesis_front.pdf

Lesh, R., & Clarke, D. (2000). Formulating operational definitions of desired outcomes of instruction in mathematics and science education. In A. Kelly & R. Lesh (Eds.), *Handbook of research design in mathematics and science education* (pp. 113–150). Mahwah, NJ: Lawrence Erlbaum.

Newton, D. (1996). Causal situations in science: A model for supporting understanding. In R. Saljo (Ed.), *Learning and Instruction* (Vol. 6(3), pp. 201–217). Great Britain: Elsevier Science Ltd.

Pratt, M. G. (2012). Rethinking identity construction processes in organizations: Three questions to consider. In M. Schultz, S. Maguire, A. Langley, & H. Tsoukas (Eds.), *Perspectives on process organization studies: Constructing identity in and around organizations* (pp. 21–49). London, UK: Oxford University Press.

Skemp, R. (1976/2006). Relational understanding and instrumental understanding. *Mathematics Teaching in the Middle School, 12*(2), 88–95. Originally published in Mathematics Teaching.

Williams, P. (2008). *Independent review of mathematics teaching in early years settings and primary schools*. Final Report. London, UK: Department for Children, Schools and Families.

Xin, Y. P., Wiles, B., & Lin, Y. (2008). Teaching conceptual model based word problem story grammar to enhance mathematics problem solving. *Journal of Special Education, 42*(3), 163–178.

5 Squaring up to the problem

A metaphor for a frontal attack!

The babble of humans communicating while collaborating is a wonderful sound; people living near schools would attest to the exuberant sound of children playing together at lunch as would those living near walking paths who often have streams of jaunty ramblers passing their house particularly during the summer. Messy problems provide opportunities for children to communicate thereby creating a babble of (working?) noise as they explore pathways towards solutions. They also enable children to be exposed to "activities out of which habits of mind might emerge" (Askew, 2015, p. 59), which means that the practices that children develop in mathematics are brought about by being involved in mathematical activity rather than learning a specific mental process. This approach can be challenging for teachers to prepare, because it means that the boundaries of generalities and definitions are extended (Askew, 2015) usually with children being engaged with others often of different abilities: reasoning becomes a collaborative mathematical activity. These problem-solving tasks can also be challenging for teachers because they require children to work in groups to produce one group artifact rather than children working together but with each creating an individual output. While the discussion of how to engage children to work cooperatively is not the focus of this text, the necessity of children being able to function productively in groups is key for many successful problem-solving activities. Humans don't spontaneously collaborate, although some individuals seem to have more skill at team or group work than others. We would suggest that you develop children's mental models of effective group work early in the year if they appear to be unproductive at producing group artifacts in lessons. Appendix 2 has an outline of an approach (4R Approach) we have used with different groups and, when used systematically and patiently, such a structure will enable all children to develop functional mental models of working in groups. So assuming that your class is at the 'functional' stage of collaborative group work, we have included this messy problem that engages children by enabling them to understand and interpret requirements of a task that is messy to start with but concludes with a 'neat' solution.

The context: a design challenge!

Design challenges are a favourite hook for Primary children particularly if instigated by someone in authority or someone who is respected by the group. We often use the principal or head teacher to instigate design challenges because doing so adds *gravitas* to the activity.

The requirements for *squaring up to the problem* in terms of knowledge of vocabulary and processes are not complicated, but the constraints embedded in the task will offer challenges that may make some children squirm with the delight of being so positioned while making others feel confused and overwhelmed. The advantage of working in mixed-ability groups is that there will be others in the groups who are able to both interpret the requirements and find ways of incorporating the constraints. We will demonstrate points at which teachers can use the Mode typology to question children if they are 'stuck' for further ideas.

This activity is designed for Key Stage 2 (10- to 11-year-old) children and can be used over, at least, two lessons depending on both the age and also the experience of the children as well as the length of the lesson periods. We have included some resource sheets in the Appendices that will be useful for the "*I can* . . ." statements, and there are several tables in the text that outline planning guidelines for teachers. This guidance is important because problem solving is of greater benefit to children if they already have certain skills necessary for completion of the task. While you will want to challenge them cognitively, it is better to ensure any supplementary skills have been mastered so as to not cause too much disequilibrium. I know that I had to master the art of casting a fly line in my back garden before I ventured into a stream wearing 'wellies' when I first went fly-fishing!

The task

You may wish to bring the principal or head teacher in to deliver the design challenge, but we would recommend that you also have the requirements on a chart or board in the room and written on handouts for the groups. The task is:

Squaring up to the problem

New School Badge

Our school needs a new badge. But there are some design specs that will reduce costs and ensure the new badge fits on our existing school uniform.

1   *The logo to go on the badge will have a line of symmetry, so to accommodate the logo the design must have at least one line of symmetry.*

2   *In order to minimize wastage of the expensive badge material the shape should tessellate.*

3   *Since the outline of the badge will be sewn onto the school jacket, it will be quicker and cheaper if the perimeter of the shape is as small as possible.*

The challenge involves children being able to enact the skills shown in Table 5.1. The sharing of some of these skills will work well with the *4R Approach* to cooperative group work (see Appendix 2), but it is important to have a clear understanding of what you will expect the children to *do* during the problem-solving experience.

Squaring up to the problem is clearly a 'bolt-on' activity because it is a 'big' challenge that requires at least two lessons of some duration. The teaching emphasis is on the application of mathematical content such as symmetry, shapes, tessellations, perimeter and area in order to develop mathematical processes in a systematic way to meet set criteria. This activity creates the opportunity for children to increase, evaluate and refine their problem-solving skills through the selection and application of mathematical knowledge and organizational and communication skills. The skills outlined in Table 5.1 start with verbs such as those discussed earlier, where Pretz, Naples and Sternberg (2003) approached the problem-solving process in an iterative way that asks learners to evaluate their progress throughout the activity using verbs such as 'recognizing' and 'developing'. Here we have used verbs in a similar way to Anderson and

Table 5.1 Skills involved in squaring up to the problem

Squaring up to the problem involves
Cutting, rearranging and gluing paper shapes;
Recognizing tessellating of shapes;
Finding symmetry of shapes;
Organizing and presenting ideas and examples;
Drawing and measuring to find lengths;
Using rules (formula) to calculate perimeters and areas;
Finding the biggest and smallest possible perimeters of a shape with the same area;
Exploring relationships between a fixed area and different perimeters;
Being creative, logical and systematic; and,
Convincing others about ideas and answers!

Krathwohl (2001), who revised Bloom's (1956) taxonomy using his higher levels such as analyzing and evaluating to prompt children with questions. They also encouraged children to use diagrams and words as well as numbers because doing so enabled the children to become better problem solvers. This task incorporates skills such as drawing and organizing shapes, thereby inducing children to think creatively while planning approaches to design, test and evaluate their solutions.

Curriculum links

The mathematical conceptual, propositional and procedural knowledge that children will be using in this activity can be related to the national curriculum in England and Wales (DfE, 2013) in several strands in upper Key Stage 2, which covers Years Five and Six (ages 9–11 years). The preamble for this stage suggests that

> teaching in geometry and measures should consolidate and extend knowledge developed in number. Teaching should also ensure that pupils classify shapes with increasingly complex geometric properties and that they learn the vocabulary they need to describe them.
>
> (DfE, 2013, p. 30)

There is a specific emphasis on the attributes of shape, but the integration of so many different strands in this activity provides ample opportunity to visit and revisit certain processes such as calculation of perimeter. The calculation of area is less of a concern because the size of the squared paper remains constant, so there is no repetition of calculation. Year Five statutory requirements state that learners will need to "measure and calculate the perimeter of composite rectilinear shapes in centimetres and metres" (DfE, 2013, p. 36). Year Six requirements state that learners will "recognise that shapes with the same areas can have different perimeters and vice versa" (DfE, 2013, p. 43). Each of these requirements is a significant aspect of this activity, but there are many opportunities for children to review much of the previous knowledge in measurement as they proceed through the lessons. Geometry also features significantly, and Year Five offers suggestions in the statutory and non-statutory guidance such as learners "use the term diagonal and make conjectures about the angles formed between sides . . . and other properties of quadrilaterals" (DfE, 2013, p. 37) and being able to "distinguish between regular and irregular polygons based on reasoning about equal sides and angles" (DfE, 2013, p. 37). Year Six also has useful guidance in the geometry statutory and non-statutory notes with suggestions that learners will "compare and classify geometric shapes based on their properties and sizes and find unknown angles in any triangles, quadrilaterals, and regular polygons" (DfE, 2013, p. 44). While

Squaring up to the problem

there are no specific requirements in the criteria to measure angles, the necessity to do so may arise when learners are exploring the symmetrical properties of the shapes.

While symmetry is part of the Year Four curriculum in which learners will "identify lines of symmetry in 2-D shapes presented in different orientations" (DfE, 2013, p. 28) the topic continues to feature in subsequent years in the form of reflections and translations around axes on coordinate planes in Year Six. Such manipulation of shape is fundamental to the development of sound algebraic knowledge, which you would have read about in Chapter 4. Recording the explorations is also vital, so aspects of statistics are also covered in this activity particularly where learners will "complete, read and interpret information in tables" (DfE, 2013, p. 38) in Year Five while also deciding "which representations of data are most appropriate and why" (DfE, 2013, p. 38). The Year Six statistics guidance suggests that learners "draw graphs relating two variables, arising from their own enquiry" (DfE, 2013, p. 45), which is a necessary aspect of recording their results when moving the diagonal cuts on the shape. *Squaring up to the problem* offers a significant opportunity for children to consolidate knowledge across the mathematics curriculum while also developing other essential skills such as collaborating, analyzing, evaluating and justifying.

There is some preparation to do for this activity, and ensuring that resources are well laid out, accessible and plentiful will ensure that the children do not have limitations imposed on their creativity due to a lack of materials. We suggest you ensure the materials in Table 5.2 are provided for the children.

Lesson 1

To get started you will need to set the scene, so copies of the task should be available for each group as well as having one on a class chart or on a digital presentation. Children may need clarification of the task, so we have found it useful to have some badge designs on hand both in a physical sense (turning them over in your hands is very useful for children who prefer tactile stimuli) and pictorially, perhaps digitally given

Table 5.2 Materials for squaring up to the problem

Materials for each group
Task outline
Coloured squared paper 6cm × 6cm (for cutting and rearranging)
Plain paper (for recording)
Scissors, glue, pencil, ruler (to work out perimeters and areas)
Calculator for using formulae (to work out perimeters and areas)
Graph paper (for plotting changes in perimeters in relation to a particular area)

the prevalence of Smart Boards™. Displays of children's work in classrooms are an important part of sharing both the learning journey and the result of effort. This activity does lend itself to such presentation, and teachers may feel it appropriate to have a *Problem-solving* board on which these activities are put on display. When introducing the design activity it's important to stress the expense of the material that will be used to make the actual badge, because it is the prudent use of such expensive material that substantiates the need for a tessellating shape that has both a good area and the smallest possible perimeter. Teachers who engage in cross-curricula activities may find this activity lends itself well to an exploration of materials and sustainability. We have found quite a few useful badge designs on the Internet, and the variety available provides useful discussion points for the children and encourage them to share badge designs they have seen, logos they remember from other contexts and the materials that they have been made from.

Enabling

This problem offers a broad problem to start working on, which pupils may find complex due to the three very clear criteria that have to be considered. It is the teacher's responsibility to creatively plan to clarify and communicate these criteria, which are, in some ways, limits and constraints that need to be understood and conformed to within the problem. As part of the teacher's presentation of this challenge, there should be opportunities that allow learners to interpret, prioritize, sort, arrange and organize information. For example, it is essential that pupils are encouraged to collaborate and discuss while working with shared resources as they work toward a shared artifact.

One of the ways that a teacher will enable children to approach this problem is to use pieces of 6cm × 6cm squared paper to demonstrate how a different shape with the same area could be made. She could use a visualizer to cut squares into two halves with a:

a   diagonal line (into two triangles); and,
b   vertical line (into two rectangles) as shown in Figure 5.1.

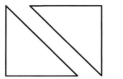
a. diagonal line creating 2 triangles

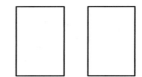
b. vertical line creating 2 rectangles

Figure 5.1 Positioning paper for demonstration of cuts

Squaring up to the problem

While repositioning the pieces that have been cut, the teacher is demonstrating some of the basic ways that shapes can be made and providing an opportunity to recap relevant vocabulary that the learners will need when discussing their options in their groups. She should also demonstrate and encourage children to talk about the

a   dimensions of each composite shape;
b   total area of each composite shape;
c   special names for particular shapes; and,
d   symmetry of shapes.

Such discussion reinforces the children's ideas about conservation of area and enables them to see the relationships between area and perimeters.

The focus of this first lesson is shapes, and their initial challenge is to explore the range of badge designs that it is possible to create from the given dimensions of the squared paper. The teacher would need to explain that their work, and ideas need to show that they have:

a   thought about their work and planned it carefully;
b   been inventive and tried a range of different ideas;
c   been logical in their approach to designing possible shapes; and,
d   clearly organized their work and findings.

The activity necessitates the children sharing their thinking, which means that they will be engaging in externalizing their mental models about shapes, badges and the attributes of the design. In this first lesson, it is essential to direct the children's work, so stopping the class to discuss their discoveries and ideas will help the teacher to focus attention on those ideas that are providing suitable attendance to the criteria and the appropriate use of language essential to explaining, predicting and diagnosing the quality of the work.

As the children share their work in this first lesson, they should be creating and recording the following shapes for which they can provide names. They will create the following shapes from cutting the initial shape into triangles:

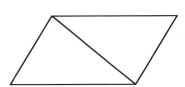 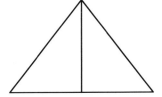

And the following shapes will be created from cutting the initial shape into rectangles.

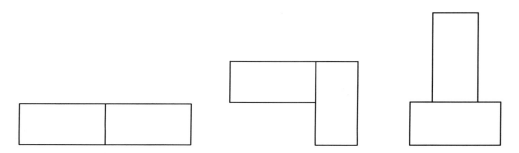

At this point suggesting that the groups tabulate their findings will promote better organizational skills and enable them to plan for extending their investigations into using other diagonal lines that cut the square into two equal trapeziums. If too much freedom in how the cuts are made occurs, the teacher can add another criteria: designs need to be joined along sides of equal length. Such guidance will ensure that the shape meets the symmetry criterion.

Lesson 2: engaging

The first lesson should have hooked the children into the idea of exploring shapes in order to design a badge that meets definitive criteria for purposes of sustainability (cost and material use). Lesson 2, which should take place in the next mathematics lesson, will enable children to be more autonomous in their inquiry, with the teacher taking a more facilitating or supporting role. The Mode Typology questions based on explaining, predicting and diagnosing will be of use at this point with groups or individuals who are struggling to move forward in the investigation or are having trouble recording their findings. At key points the teacher may stop the class for a sharing or question point in order that progress can be evaluated by each group. Such mini plenary sessions, as they are often called, offer the opportunity to focus the learners on the requirements of the task and to share artifacts that demonstrate correct responses to the requirements of the task. We feel they are key times when children can exercise their skill with the vocabulary to explain the processes they have been using to find solutions, so teachers should be mindful of not doing all of the talking themselves: children need opportunities to explain their efforts, so ensure plenary sessions focus on the learners doing the talking.

Explaining prompts can include such questions as, *How can you explain what you are finding?* and "*Can you demonstrate your findings by comparing the different results?* The use of diagrams to illustrate the differences in the criteria, particularly the perimeter lengths, is important at this point, and guidance from the national curriculum (DfE, 2013) is useful, prompting teachers to ensure children have the opportunity to compare and classify shapes in particular ways. The use of a physical artifact ensures the children are using appropriate descriptive vocabulary in their communication. It is during the mini plenary sessions that the predictive prompts can be used with groups who may be stalled in their enquiry process. Prompts such as, *What do you think will be the result if you move the diagonal across another centimetre?* will encourage groups to venture further in their enquiry and promote such questions to the class, thereby establishing such questions as part of the normative process of problem solving. Prediction for other results or next steps can also be encouraged or guided by asking, *What can you use this information (moving the diagonal across 1cm) to do next?* which stimulates the children to look beyond one discovery to anticipate what they might do next in their enquiry. The prompts are designed to focus children on both what they have discovered and also what they are yet to find. They ensure that the teacher fulfils their role as facilitator who understands that there are ways of taking our knowledge further rather than assessor or arbiter who is satisfied when children have reached one particular step only.

The design brief and its parameters need to be revisited at the beginning of the second lesson and an abundance of paper provided for the groups. The focus in this lesson is less on shape and more on the need to minimize the perimeter. So you will have questions to the children about other ways of cutting the shape in half in order to establish the notion of gradually moving from cutting corner to corner to cutting vertically. Some of the resulting shapes are shown in what follows, where cuts are made 1cm from the top corner to 1cm from the bottom and then shifting to 2cm and so on. Engagement comes from encouraging the children to think about ways of finding the sloping edges of the perimeters and the effect on the perimeter in relation to the area. The focus of children's work will be about finding the lengths and areas of shapes:

a   counting squares;

b   using their own rules; and,

c   using taught rules/formulae.

Estimation and measuring should be encouraged and used as a comparison and will lead into the teacher introducing Pythagoras' Theorem, where:

> *The sum of the squares on the two shorter sides of a right-angled triangle equal the square on the longest (hypotenuse) sides or* $a^2 + b^2 = h^2$

> *Example: The length of diagonal in a 6cm square is: $6^2 + 6^2 = $ diagonal 2cm*
> *So, 36 + 36 = diagonal 2cm*
> *Which means 72 = diagonal 2cm*
> *And therefore 8.5cm = diagonal.*

It is important to encourage accurate measurement and recording of lengths, so providing a good stock of rulers is necessary, as is skill in using them accurately. Indeed, the emphasis on accuracy is a key step for children as they develop their knowledge of measurement. We have used the centimetre as the measurement value in this activity, although there is some value in encouraging children in Key Stage 2 (9–11 years) to move towards the use of millimetres. Millimetres are the measure of choice in the real world of measurement, particularly in building trades, due in part to the millimetre being the smallest standard measure visible to the 'naked' human eye. The centimetre is rarely used outside the classroom: televisions are measured corner to corner in inches, turf is measured by metres, and ready-made curtains are measured in centimetres. On the Internet, the description for a particular brand of skateboard used the following measures:

> A 7-ply maple 31″ [inch] deck with a double kick, concave shape, a stylised Ridge graphic to the underside and 5″ aluminium raw trucks with a 5mm riser pad. The 50mm x 36mm PU wheels and fitted sealed bearings are made for riding on hard concrete surfaces, making it perfect for parks and pools.
> (www.skatehut.co.uk/ridge_double_kick_ trick_complete_skateboard_7_75.htm)

The use of disparate imperial (inches) and metric (millimetres) measures has obviously been unproblematic for the creator of the description and, perhaps, may emanate from long-established norms in construction. Timber lengths, at major suppliers in the UK, are presented in millimetres, so the 31-inch maple deck of the skateboard is antithetical to the current protocols. But you can purchase ready-made fence panels measured in feet from the same supplier, so there is little consistency in the use of measures. So teachers need to be comfortable working in both imperial and metric measures to the extent that they can encourage the children they are working with to be the same. Normative behaviour will not disappear from commerce regardless of the Treaty of Accession to the European Economic Community in 1973, which started the journey toward full metrification and is likely to meet further resistance as the UK moves towards Brexit. For a historic view of the use of imperial and metric measures in industry, a read of the Cockcroft Report (Cockcroft, 1982, p. 24) discusses pragmatic reasons such as the cost to recalibrate machinery and of re-equipping workshops as being significant influences of the continued use of a range of measures.

Evaluating

The groups will establish that ensuring they have a persistent application of strategies their engagement will be purposeful throughout the problem-solving process. The purpose of engaging in *squaring up to the problem* will impact on the role of the teacher throughout and particularly as they approach the evaluating stage in which the groups will be working toward a narrowing set of solutions. The process of *evaluating* will involve pupils testing, recording and subsequently explaining their possible solutions. Here the teacher's role will be to challenge the groups to support the appropriateness and quality of their solutions; the groups will need to justify their selections, which will require them to be convinced about the efficiency of the processes they have used and the effectiveness of such processes to find a solution that meets all criteria.

One way that the teacher can encourage children to explore the impact of using diagonal lines to cut squares is to show the result of length changes on a graph. Figure 5.2 illustrates the type of graph that groups should be creating as they alter the distance from the corners for each subsequent cut.

The groups should be able to discuss their findings in relation to how they have plotted the results on the graph, which provides information about the possible cuts. Fractional lengths of cuts have been included, but the learners will be able to read between the calculated results to find lengths of cut 1.5cm and 2.5cm from the corners. The graph allows children to prove that the diagonal from corner to corner is the

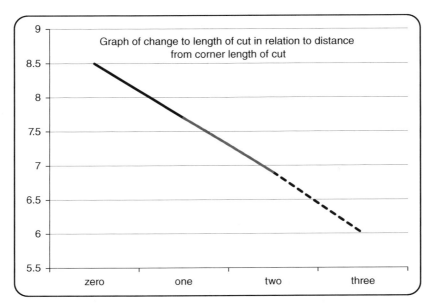

Figure 5.2 Graph showing how length of cut changes in relation to distance from corner

longest length, and such understanding will enable them to better select the shape that provides the shortest perimeter as required by the task design criteria.

Evaluating all possible shapes that the children would have created during both Lesson 1 and 2 against the design criteria is now essential in order that the groups can select their best badge design. The evaluation involves children reasoning, which as Askew (2015, p. 59) can become "hidden to us when ideas are very familiar", which they would have become to the children in the groups as they worked together to arrive at a solution. Askew (2015) refers to reasoning as an internal micro-activity, which can be an extended process if the problem to be solved is difficult or complex. The national curriculum (DfE, 2013) features reasoning throughout the strands and year levels and refers to it as a thinking process that is developed in order to analyze, describe, make connections and find results.

You may wish to provide some good-quality card, perhaps in a metallic finish, so that the 'best' result from each group can be prepared for the final plenary session. What you would expect to see, in preparation for the final selection, is that each group has tabulated their findings in such a way that the best fit for the design is obvious. Table 5.3 shows one layout of a table that the children might come up with in order to evaluate their designs. We have seen quite a few different approaches to this evaluation process and feel that it is often best that the groups discover a process for themselves. Once the final plenary session is complete, they will have been exposed to several ways of evaluating, and you can use this information for another mathematics lesson on how we can organize data to efficiently and effectively evaluate data.

Recording shapes in this way will enable the groups to expose each shape they have created to the scrutiny embedded in the criteria. A complete set of answers is provided in Appendix 3 so that teachers can see the full set of artefacts and guide the groups to explore more widely if their results show limitations. The descriptors present in each shape also offer fodder for further lessons, with opportunities to explore

Table 5.3 Recording of shapes

Shape	Name	Tessellate?	Lines of symmetry	Order of rotational symmetry	Matching edge	Perimeter (cm to 1dp)	Area (cm²)
	Square	Yes	4	4	Diagonal or vertical	24	36
	Parallelogram	Yes	0	2	6cm side	29	36
	Isosceles Triangle	Yes	1	1	6cm side	29	36

the differences between concave pentagons and convex pentagons. Some interesting shapes such as the bow hexagon and pin hexagon will provide significant windows through which you can explore shapes with the children. Such names or labels place the focus on the attributes of shape because the names derive from certain characteristics which are linked to particular properties. Developing children's vocabulary so that they can communicate well mathematically is essential in developing their confidence to participate in problem-solving activities and investigations.

In summary

The final plenary session should showcase the children's evaluation of their results, and the nominated responder (see *4R Approach* in Appendix 2) will present their justifications for selection and try to convince the audience about the efficiency of their approach and the appropriateness and quality of their solution. What is most likely in this session is that all groups would have arrived at one of two options: the isosceles trapezium or the parallelogram, with both having a diagonal cut 2cm from the corners (see Appendix 3 for a full set of results). Both of these shapes meet all criteria with the same shortest perimeter of 26.4cm, they both tessellate, and each has different symmetrical properties: the isosceles trapezium has both 1 line of symmetry and rotational symmetry of order 1, while the parallelogram has no lines of symmetry but has rotational symmetry of order 2. If a group has selected a shape that has a longer perimeter than 26.4cm such as that for an isosceles trapezium with a diagonal cut 1cm from the corners and reaching 27.6cm in perimeter, then that group would need to defend their decision to exceed the length by 1.2cm for each shape. Their response may not be technically acceptable, but the more elongated shape may have other aesthetic qualities that mitigate the need for a shorter perimeter: such is the humanness of mathematics and the idiosyncratic mental models that each of us have when selecting designs that are pleasing.

References

Anderson, L. W., & Krathwohl, D. R. (2001). *A taxonomy for learning, teaching, and assessing: A revision of Bloom's taxonomy of educational objectives.* London, UK: Longman.

Askew, M. (2015). *Transforming primary mathematics: Understanding classroom tasks, tools and talk.* Oxon, UK: Routledge.

Bloom, B. S. (Ed.). (1956). *Taxonomy of educational objectives, the classification of educational goals – handbook I: Cognitive domain.* New York, NY: McKay.

Cockcroft, W. H. (1982). *The Cockcroft report: Mathematics counts*, Report of the Committee of Inquiry into the teaching of mathematics in schools. London, UK: Her Majesty's Stationery Office.

Department for Education (2013). *The national curriculum for England and Wales.* London, UK: DfE.

Pretz, J. E., Naples, A. J., & Sternberg, R. J. (2003). Recognizing, defining, and representing problems. In J. E. Davidson & R. J. Sternberg (Eds.), *The psychology of problem solving* (pp. 3–30). Cambridge: Cambridge University Press.

6 | Rich tasks and big questions

A bit of background

The title of this chapter makes reference to an initiative of Education Queensland who launched the New Basics Trial (2000–2004) introducing three suites of Rich Tasks that covered three 3-year spans from Year One (ages 5–6) to Year Nine (ages 13–14). The Rich Tasks at the centre of the New Basics Trial were "rich in the sense of having variety, scope and depth; in requiring academic rigour; and in being multidisciplinary" (Matters, 2006, p. 18). The New Basics approach to curriculum differed from a subject-based or key-learning-areas approach and was taught in "four categories of essential practices for new times: Life pathways and social futures, Multiliteracies and communications 'media, Active citizenship, and Environments and technologies" (Matters, 2006, p. 19). Of the 38 schools that started the trial in 2000, after 3 years one had dropped out and another 22 had joined, indicating the increased popularity of it in schools. The tasks at the heart of the approach provided opportunities for students to engage in extended performance tasks that combined subject areas and were sensitive to local school-specific and community needs. The tasks were very specific activities that students undertook and had real-world value or were what Askew (2012) called connectivist by nature, ultimately allowing students to demonstrate their grasp and use of knowledge and ideas as well as the skills necessary to investigate and communicate. We would suggest that the tasks enabled the students to develop functional mental models that were rich in networks of related understandings.

While we are not proposing to adopt such a radical change to curriculum construction here, there are features of such a framework that can be adopted in Primary classrooms particularly when teachers are seeking to embrace a problem-solving approach to learning. Such approaches, sometimes couched in terms of 'cross-curricula', mirror our lives; there is very little that we do in 'real life' that focuses on only one aspect of knowledge for any length of time. When I'm cooking a meal I am not simply heating food; I am measuring, timing, tasting, combining, counting cutlery, gauging heat from the gas hob, stepping over the cat and considering what's for pudding, all while the vegetables are steaming. When students are undertaking Rich Tasks they are not being taught one subject by just one teacher or remaining in the confines of one classroom for any length of time. The experience provides a "real-world context within which to extend, bring together and display high-level knowledge of various disciplines" (Grauf, 2001, p. 4). A Rich Tasks require students to

> solve problems, be critical and analytical thinkers and use the knowledge and skills they have acquired in a variety of contexts in a variety of ways. The Rich Tasks also require students to associate new learning with that which is already known, to have a clear statement of expectations and realise that their knowledge can be transferred to new situations.
>
> (Grauf, 2001, p. 5)

None of the above is necessarily novel in its approach, because all around the world many teachers challenge children with activities that require them to be critical and to build new knowledge on that which is already known. This requirement of a learning task and its associated pedagogical approach is one that most educators would see as value and necessary for the preparation of students to be capable citizens in our ever-changing world. Such an approach also recognizes the understandings, or mental models, that students have developed in their 'real' lives by suggesting that "knowledge and skills they have acquired in a variety of contexts and a variety of ways" (Grauf, 2001, p. 5) are to be used in a critical way when engaging in learning. This explicit acknowledgement of the idiosyncratic nature of knowledge has significant implications for the teachers who are interested in exploring problem-solving or investigative approaches with their students. The third aspect of the New Basics Trial offers ideas for teachers of Primary mathematics.

A third aspect of the New Basics Trial was the third arm of the initiative called Productive Pedagogies, which are "classroom strategies that teachers can use to focus instruction and improve student outcomes" (Grauf, 2001, p. 8). It is here we see strong connections to the Primary mathematics curriculum (DfE, 2013) through the focus on such things as higher-order thinking, deep knowledge and understanding and problem-base curriculum. While other aspects of Productive Pedagogies go beyond the explicit remit of the mathematics curriculum (DfE, 2013) such as the inclusion of cultural knowledges and active citizenship (Grauf, 2001), there are many similarities in how we would like to see learning approached in Primary mathematics classrooms through self-regulatory practice, explicit quality performance criteria and student direction (Grauf, 2001). Matters (2006) suggests that Rich Tasks within the New Basic Trials embedded with Productive Pedagogical approaches provide children with clear guidelines for what they'll be learning and how they will be assessed while constantly being "encouraged to take risks in a safe environment and be responsible for their own behaviour and learning" (p. 24). Most teachers would want their classroom to be what Goleman, Boyatzis and McKee (2002) call a safe place for learning; a place where children have the opportunity to explore new ideas, build upon existing understandings and critique their world. Interpretations of the term 'rich task' make for more plausible development of the approach in Primary mathematics classrooms, which continue to embrace the ethos of the phenomena without requiring a complete overhaul of the curriculum. We feel that these approaches are worth reviewing before we move on to suggested activities.

Rich tasks in mathematics

Griffin (2009), writing for the Association of Teachers of Mathematics (ATM) in the UK, described rich tasks as "tasks that when mediated in certain ways produce certain kinds of actions and mathematical behaviours in our learners" (p. 32). But he warns that the task itself is not the only necessary ingredient for a challenging and stimulating learning environment. Griffin (2009) refers to the culture of the room, in which meta-cognition and the awareness of how the students influence everything they do enables them to work *on* tasks that result from questions aimed to find out what they are thinking with the genuine goal of assessing their own thoughts. Material produced by NRICH (2008) reflects this thinking about rich tasks, posing the idea that while the tasks should provide opportunity for both higher- and lower-order thinking, they remain problems because there is a gap between what is known and what needs to be known. Filling the gap requires thinking and playing because "by playing with the mathematics, patterns and connections often reveal themselves" (NRICH, 2008, p. 6). The richness, they suggest, comes from "what happens next . . . ideas begin to emerge from playing with the initial situation and sometimes from posing problems of their own" (NRICH, 2008, p. 6). The reference to 'play' returns our thinking to Zeeman's delightful and illuminating recommendation for engaging children in mathematics through play, signifying that there is indeed a philosophical consideration required when we embark on teaching mathematics, and perhaps that remains the best position from which to interrogate our planning for learning.

Big questions

One way to begin to immerse a classroom of children into rich tasks that enable them to play with mathematics in a safe environment while meeting the demands of any mathematics curriculum is to ask big questions. We don't mean *long, complicated* questions. *Big* questions enable idiosyncratic investigations in which students are required to draw on many types of knowledge at different times and at different rates in order to satisfy the difference between what is known at the beginning, what is found during the investigation and what has been learnt throughout. *Big* questions can be quite short. The one we will explore here for its possibilities in a Primary mathematics classroom is, "What is the best cup of coffee?"

The takeaway coffee culture of most Western countries has resulted in increased public discussion of sustainability issues around paper cup production and recycling (see Rustin, 2016, *The Guardian*, March 16, 2016) as well as larger economic issues to do with taxation of companies (see Davies, 2015, *The Guardian*, December 15, 2015). The industry has also spawned a whole new culture and language based on products (latte, macchiato) and producers (baristas, cafetière), let alone the names of the countless sizes of cups that have emerged from a variety of coffee chains and franchises. The coffee culture, while in some ways being a few years in the future for most of our Primary students, infiltrates their lives in many ways and offers teachers opportunities to explore the phenomenon using a 'critical literacy' or critical pedagogy approach.

Critical literacy, first posited by the New London Group (1996) in furthering Freire's (1972) and Freire and Macedo's (1987) political stance and pedagogical perspectives on education, engages the learner in looking for patterns in the world, the system designs that are used for everyday life, how complex the interrelationships are between such patterns and systems and their impact on our lives. The action that students engage in is not only the recognition of such patterns and relationships but also understanding that they can redesign and shape it. Luke (2012, p. 9) suggests that how teachers "shape and deploy the tools, attitudes, philosophies of critical literacy is utterly contingent: It depends upon students' and teachers' everyday relations of power, their lived problems and struggles" and also how teachers engage creatively with contexts to create stimulating and 'real' opportunities for learning. While the critical literacy approach has a seminal focus on texts in which the ideological contents as well as the lexico-grammatical structures (Luke, 2012) are explored and understood for how multiple texts will position a reader, we can argue that there is also a significant opportunity for a critical numeracy approach. Using critical numeracy approaches would entail the exploration of social and economic phenomena so that children begin to understand how mathematics is used in social functions to position consumers, often through tactics such as confusion marketing (two-for-one deals), for economic purposes. As we discuss this big question, we will offer examples of how teachers can include such useful, and some would say necessary, elements of criticality into their teaching.

I asked a simple question about coffee when I was working in a school in East London. My arrival at school each morning with a cup of coffee from a notable franchise prompted the children I was teaching to ask me what type of coffee it was. I told them it was a black Americano coffee and boasted it was the best one to drink.

Rich tasks and big questions

A couple of children countered my claim by saying that their parents regularly drank a different type of coffee from a different coffee shop and that theirs was the *best* coffee. I replayed the conversation in class one day, asking the children which *was* the best cup of coffee. Given our location near a notable business district there was a variety of franchises, chains, and independent coffee shops, which most children were aware of and had their (or their parents') opinions of. The big question started a chain of inquiry that was quite breath-taking in its impact on learning. Parents became involved, as did other teachers in the school, as the children in my class sought different ways of determining an answer. What follows is an explanation of how such a big question can prompt an investigation to solve a problem. Links to the national curriculum are shown, as are the types of prompts that I used relating to the functions of the Mental Model Mode: explaining, predicting, diagnosing and communicating.

A big question: measuring cups

Much of the mathematical activity that emerged from this big question was in the areas of measurement and statistics in Key Stage 2. Other areas of mathematics were engaged when students were required to conduct operations to add and subtract in whole and fractional (including decimal) numbers and to make proportional calculations in order to compare quantities. One of the aims of the national curriculum that was particularly relevant to the investigation was "students solving problems by applying their mathematics to . . . non-routine problems with increasing sophistication, including breaking down problems into a series of simpler steps and persevering in seeking solutions" (DfE, 2013, p. 3). The pursuit of an answer to the big question required children to plan their method of attack. I gave them little guidance at first and usually in the form of asking questions rather than providing a process to follow.

Enabling

What does the question mean we have to do?

We brainstormed the question as a class, because this was the first time the students had been exposed to such an open brief. I used the term 'brief' with them because it was an expression I had used for much of my Primary teaching in Australia, where integrated units of work were covered over a term by students through the completion of a workbook that contained a series of briefs or tasks that they were to complete. Much of this approach is demonstrated in the processes of design, make and evaluate in England's and Wales's Design and Technology curriculum (DfE, 2013), where children can be provided with a 'brief' to complete in the critique and development of an artefact, whether it be a system or a physical product.

The students were then asked to form groups of two or three to work in, because such compositions provided them with opportunities to work with friends that they liked or with someone they felt might have the skills they felt they lacked. In all but two cases, children worked in friendship groups of three; one pair worked with their teaching assistant because their needs were such that extra guidance would be useful, and another pair worked together because they liked to challenge each other with difficult mathematics problems, indicating their interdependence.

Engaging

Explaining

Students sat with their group while we had our preliminary brainstorming session, and some of the questions I used to prompt the students to start thinking about the big question included:

- What does the question say?
- What am I looking for?
- What do I already know?

The question, *What is the best cup of coffee?* was intentionally vague. Children started to question or evaluate the qualifier 'best' in their efforts to understand what actions they needed to make to solve it. Teachers need to have clarity about how they will respond to such queries, and in this case I returned the inquiries with questions indicated by the following:

Student: What do you mean by 'best'?
Teacher: What do you think 'best' means?
Student: Does it mean cheapest?
Teacher: Is the best cup of coffee the cheapest cup of coffee?

If the student responded with 'yes' to that question, then that decision would guide what they would do next and so what question would follow from me to prompt them to plan their actions.

Teacher: How might you find the cost or price of cups of coffee?
Student: You could visit the coffee shop or go online.

Suddenly, the groups that decided that this 'cost' approach would find a suitable answer had an objective and therefore could devise their strategy for finding the information necessary.

The influence of children's family and social groups was quite evident to me, if not to themselves, as they started to select which determiner of 'best' they were going to use. This is significant because if the exercise was constrained by the teacher and focused only on one determiner, it would exclude the consideration of other factors that human beings think are of greater value. Embracing the mental models of many into our investigations can offer all students the opportunity to engage in something that matters to them, that they will take with them as important concepts and that will contain the linked relational knowledge that they can call on in future to respond to problems or investigations. Jonassen (2011) discusses the importance of epistemological development and how exposure to such 'ill-defined' problems as the 'best coffee' question offered students the opportunity to progress from "simple, black and white thinking, through an exploration of multiple perspectives, to complex, relativistic thinking" (p. 23). The aims of the national curriculum (DfE, 2013), such as fluency and reasoning, are supported by epistemological development where students are able to advance their skills of judgment and reflection by considering their own and others' mental models.

Other groups of children were not quite so sure about the cheapest cup of coffee being the best cup of coffee. They understood that price mattered to some people but were concerned that the taste or style of the coffee mattered as well and would therefore trump the price consideration.

Student: Does 'best' mean the one with the nicest flavours?
Teacher: Do you think the best cup of coffee is the one that has more ingredients or tastes a certain way?
Student: What if you don't like milk?
Teacher: Do you think that the best cup of coffee has to have milk in it?

Suddenly an animated discussion followed on the merits of different styles of coffee and how different ingredients such as milk or chocolate could alter what 'best' meant when comparing coffee. The inclusion of other ingredients also returned the students to the consideration of price, because more flavours and more costly ingredients might mean the price would rise.

Teacher: How might you find the different types of coffee available?
Student: You could visit the coffee shop or go online.

Students were starting to arrive at the decision point that required them to seek more information from their environment in order to be able to answer the question. They

Rich tasks and big questions

were reaching points that also required them to consider alternative ways of collecting, collating and analyzing the information they would find. As a class we discussed that in real life, the seeking of relevant information from different sources to solve problems was an everyday occurrence. Three considerations were necessary. First was some ways of determining the correctness or truth of the information. If a student went online how could they determine if the site was reputable and therefore the information correct? We discussed how to search for sites that would be of use. Second was whether or not the information being sought and gained was sufficient for a solution to be worked out in some way. How much information was needed in order to arrive at a conclusion? Third was the consideration of how the information could be organized in such a way that it could be analyzed to find a solution. Such deliberations lead us to the next function of the Mode, predicting. However, before we move to that function, there was one more variation of the theme of *best* that arose that moved the students into different areas of the mathematics curriculum and that is worth sharing.

Two groups of students were not swayed by the focus of the best cup of coffee either being the cheapest or having the most delicious ingredients. They were convinced that 'best' meant 'most' and were interested in exploring the different sizes that coffee came in. Perhaps these students' mental models of best were shaped by their familial experiences of shopping in which prudence and good budgeting means that you need to get the most for your pound. This is a relevant and important critical numeracy opportunity and one that can shape many mathematics lessons.

Student: Does 'best' mean the most coffee in the cup? The biggest cup?
Teacher: Do you think that the best cup of coffee is the one where you get the most coffee?
Student: My mother always buys a *grande* which means small I think.
Teacher: If you were interested in the sizes of coffee cups where might you get that information?
Student: You could visit the coffee shop or go online.

And again, we arrived at a point at which students were required to gather different types of information from a variety of sources. This time the information would require students to engage in the collation of measurement information as well as the assorted names that coffee companies gave their cup sizes. Because these names were non-standard, a way of comparing measures rather than relying on names was necessary. The pursuit of all of these attributes of 'best', price, flavour, size meant that the students' investigations were bound to become more engaging through the complexity of the information they would both come across and also sift for use. '*Bigger than Ben Hur*' was a phrase that started to go through my mind at this point – but I chose not to share that thought with the students.

96

Enacting

Action (play?)

The students made a commitment to their investigations, and we made use of the room's computer, which was connected to the internet, to search for websites of the major coffee chains and franchises as well as any other coffee shops in the local community. One of the teaching assistants monitored the students' use of the computer to ensure they remained focused and didn't get distracted as they sought the information for the investigation. The students had very clear ideas of what knowledge they would be seeking but very little idea about how they would be organizing it at this stage. Their mental models of such processes were naïve at best, and while they had been exposed to mathematics activities that required them to sort information and present it systematically in tables or graphs, they had never before started from such a unknown point, because teachers had invariably provided the information, the structure to sort it, the process to interrogate it and an expectation of how it would be presented at the end. These experiences are necessary for students to gain an understanding of the importance of handling data well but did not provide such opportunities for such a rich experience as sorting data on coffee! Most of all, teachers usually model the processes that they require students to use when they introduce topics such as statistics. In this case I provided none of those earlier modelling lessons or parts of lessons because of the ill-structured approach to the investigation.

In Year Three, the students had been engaged in activities in the statistics strand which required them to:

- Interpret and present data using bar charts, pictograms and tables; and,
- Solve one-step and two-step questions [for example, 'How many more?' and 'How many fewer?'] using information presented in scaled bar charts and pictograms and tables (DfE, 2013, p. 23).

So they had encountered tables, which I believe to be of most use to them in collecting and presenting the information they would be gathering for analysis. In Year Four, the curriculum required them to:

- Interpret and present discrete and continuous data using appropriate graphical methods, including bar charts and time graphs; and,
- Solve comparison, sum and difference problems using information presented in bar charts, pictograms, tables and other graphs (DfE, 2013, p. 29).

There was a very clear expectation that the students should be presenting or compiling information in ways that enabled them to interpret it and to subsequently solve

Rich tasks and big questions

problems using that information. The Coffee Cup investigation certainly enabled them to meet the requirement of the curriculum while also fulfilling its aims of:

- **reason(ing) mathematically** by following a line of enquiry, conjecturing relationships and generalisations, and developing an argument, justification or proof using mathematical language; and,
- **solving problems** by applying their mathematics to a variety of routine and non- routine problems with increasing sophistication, including breaking down problems into a series of simpler steps and persevering in seeking solutions (DfE, 2013, p. 3).

The further requirements that are outlined for Years Five and Six, in Upper Key Stage 2 of the national curriculum (DfE, 2013), do not express any more complex engagement with statistics that would inform the activity in this investigation. Year Five has a statutory requirement that students "complete, read and interpret information in tables, including timetables" and a non-statutory one that recommends "they begin to decide which representations of data are most appropriate and why" (DfE, 2013, p. 38), which has implications for this activity in that the students will be required to consider the best way to present the information they will be finding in order to solve the problem. This need to explore the ways that information is presented is very important and engages students in a critical literacy/numeracy approach that encourages them to interrogate how text can be manipulated and presented in order to influence the reader to act in a certain way. When children were collecting information from online sites and from a variety of cafés, they were exposed to many texts that were designed to invite them to act in certain ways. We started to explore these ideas as they arose, and the students were particularly intrigued by how coffee styles and sizes were named, which suggested that they were starting to 'notice' their world with more critical hats and so were in a different position to judge the value of the information they were collecting.

Before we move to the next phase of the investigation in which students started to gather the information they thought would be of use, it is important to discuss the limitations and opportunities of this style of investigation. Once students started to search online for coffee chains they knew or had seen in the local area, it soon became apparent that selecting a group of shops for the investigation was going to be necessary. We did a search online for information about the most popular coffee 'big' brands in London and found that londontoolkit.com provided a useful comparison for us to use. They listed three of the most popular brands at that time, and the students were comfortable using their recommendation because these three companies were familiar to the students and in the local area. One local shop wasn't noted because it was an independent coffee shop. Because it did sell takeaway coffee and several of

98

the parents used and valued it, the class decided that if the owner agreed to be part of the investigation we would include this café's coffee in our calculations. Therefore, once I had approached the owner and she had agreed to provide the relevant information, we commenced our data collection. While londontoolkit.com provided pricing information based on sizes (small, medium and large), I visited each of the local big brand shops to collect the information not online or in the comparison site in order to gather the information missing, which was about the various names and measures of the sizes. I drank a lot of coffee, but it was the most expeditious way to gain the information required.

Examining

Predicting

Many of the online sites for the variety of coffee shops have abundant information on the types of coffee they sell as well as the recipes they follow, their ingredients and the nutritional information. Such abundant information on the style of coffee provided those students who were interested in evaluating the merits of flavour in order to establish the 'best' coffee sufficient data to commence their investigation quite quickly. Once the students had collected their information we had a conversation:

Teacher: What can you use this information to do next?
Student: We can ask people which coffee they like?
Teacher: What do you think you need to do so you can ask them?
Student: We can have a list of coffee types for them to choose.

The students were able to spend time organizing their information in ways that enabled others to make a selection. Making predictions or test running how their instrument for collecting preferences might work was a new venture for them, so I asked them:

Teacher: What have you seen that offers people a chance to make a choice?
Student: We can give them a multiple-choice question.
Teacher: How many choices are you going to give them? (Explaining prompt)

This question, which required them to explain their process, prompted them to consider the layout of the questionnaire they were designing. Their exposure to multiple-choice questions was limited to their classroom experiences, because it is not often that students are responding to these inquiries in everyday life. In the end, the students found the list provided by londontoolkit.com to be very useful, and such a decision prompted the groups who were investigating prices to consider using the same list. Suddenly different groups were talking to each other, comparing the processes they were using and evaluating their benefits. The room was buzzing and children were making decisions, and predictions, about what was to happen next.

All of the groups finally reached a point at which they had a questionnaire to inflict on their targeted participants. While we did not address ethical considerations in depth, we did discuss the use of manners and certain protocols when conducting their survey. At this point different safe-guarding issues were also addressed, because children can be naïve in their quest for adventure, and teachers need to be aware of how to engage children in their classes in real-life surveys that don't expose them to any danger. It was also necessary to limit the timing of the surveys, because some children were so engaged that they wanted the exercise to continue well beyond a time when it was reasonable within the constraints of the investigation. All of the children were finding enjoyment in mathematics, and as Turner (2013, p. 145) suggests, "there can be no richer place than the world outside the classroom in terms of mathematics". This is what we found: most of the investigations actually occurred in the classroom, but the thinking involved and the people engaged existed in a world outside our classroom space. Suddenly, mathematics was real and 'doing maths' meant finding a solution to a question for which most people the children knew held some opinion: the children could engage in 'real' conversations and be the holders and creators of knowledge. When children had their data we moved to the next phase, in which they were now in a position to make decisions about evaluating what they had discovered.

Evaluating

Diagnosing

Diagnosis, according to Jonassen (2011), is often a process of pattern recognition and this would certainly be the case when students are undertaking investigations such as consecutive sums (see Chapter 4). In the Coffee Cup investigation the diagnostic function is more reliant on the student understanding or evaluating whether they have sufficient information to either act successfully as they move forward (so therefore they are diagnosing continuously) or to complete the investigation and offer a solution or result. Being busy on a project when you know that you have the right tools, equipment, materials and time to complete it well is very satisfying, and the hum that comes from busy, productive classrooms is because students are, if not already at an equilibrium or unperturbed state, then at least in the act of moving towards one. What you would expect to see and hear at this stage of the investigation is what Turner (2013, p. 36) calls a "symbiosis between numerical skills, problem-solving and investigative

Rich tasks and big questions

skills". She believes that this "process requires a sense of imagination and curiosity as well as knowledge of number skills" (Turner, 2013, p. 36), and we would agree that the curiosity that drove the students in this investigation is vital to strengthen their attitudes of competence and confidence of being learners and of being investigators.

Most of the prompts that I used at this stage of the investigations were about process.

Teacher: Why did you collect this information?
Student: It tells us what the people like to drink, the flavours they like.
Teacher: Why has this information been useful?
Student: Because we can count how many of each flavour they like and see which one is the best.

The 'why' questions associated with diagnosing the usefulness of their strategies and the value of the information they have found is fundamental in encouraging them to interrogate what it means in terms of responding to the big question.

In this investigation all groups 'solved' the problem and provided a result in one form or another. Once the groups were calculating their responses to the 'best' coffee question, several students were interested in how they should present their findings. During a whole-class discussion we returned to the *explaining* function of mental models, and I asked how they could explain what they found. I also used a *communicating* prompt to ask, Could you convince someone about what you found? Some of the students had rich data about the different types, prices and sizes of coffee preferred by the people they asked. The numbers for each group were different but not too dissimilar due to the availability of family members, neighbours and staff at the school willing to participate in the questionnaires. We moved to statistics once more to explore the possibilities for presenting the data we had collected and to see if we could reach some conclusions about what the best cup of coffee looked like.

Communicating

What did you learn in school today? On the final day of our investigations, the results of the big question, *What is the best cup of coffee?* were presented to the class. We ensured there was sufficient time for all groups to present their findings and to communicate what they had found out, how they had found it and why they had conducted the investigations the way that they had. Most presentations took a couple of minutes, so it's important to ensure you stagger these throughout a session to ensure all children remain focused. We had 10 presentations in all, reasonably well spread over the three attributes flavour, price and size. Students also chose different graphical

101

forms to present their results, and while the appropriateness of the selected format was of interest and something to interrogate, it did not drive the activity. The students' drive and ability to communicate what they had learned, how they had found out and what they now understood was the most valued outcome. It's important that teachers don't alter the intention of the activity and evolve it into something that becomes a measurable task rather than a pleasurable activity.

Moving forward

Jonassen (2011) provided us with some useful commentary when discussing investigations such as coffee cups. He said, "the situatedness of the instruction facilitates comprehension, retention, recognition of the conditions in which learning may be applied and therefore transferred" (Jonassen, 2011, p. 163). The skills that the students developed through this activity were applied to an authentic task because the scenario was both realistic and also shared with their community. It was plausible and offered a meaningful and achievable goal, and the skills they had learned were portable. Appreciating the students' different mental models meant that they had the autonomy to select the attribute they had most in common with to drive their investigation. I provided the sounding board, the guide on the side, who prompted them with questions so that they could squirm their way to a decision because they were obliged to respond, to react with intention, to make a decision. I trusted them with the decision-making process and monitored their progress at each step of that process. I have confidence that I enabled their mental models of investigating such issues to be strengthened and enriched because they were in a safe place to do so. While the prices have increased since the time this investigation was completed with the children, the flavour and size of cup would probably hold some ground. The 'best' cup of coffee, by unanimous vote from the staff, mums and dads in the area was a small black Americano! I crowed for a week!

References

Askew, M. (2012). *Transforming primary mathematics*. Oxon, UK: Routledge.

Davies, R. (2015). Starbucks pays UK corporation tax of £8.1m. *The Guardian*. Retrieved December 15, 2015, from www.theguardian.com/business/2015/dec/15/starbucks-pays-uk-corporation-tax-8-million-pounds

Department for Education (2013). *The national curriculum for England and Wales*. London, UK: DfE.

Freire, P. (1972). *Pedagogy of the oppressed*. London, UK: Penguin Books.

Freire, P., & Macedo, D. (1987). *Literacy: Reading the word and the world*. South Hadley, MA: Bergin & Garvey.

Goleman, D., Boyatzis, R., & McKee, A. (2002). *The new leaders: Transforming the art of leadership with the science of results*. London, UK: Time-Warner.

Grauf, E. (2001). *New basics: Queensland trials a curriculum for tomorrow*. Brisbane: Education Queensland.

Griffin, P. (2009). What makes a rich task? In *Mathematics teaching* (pp. 32–34). Derby, UK: ATM.

Jonassen, D. H. (2011). *Learning to solve problems: A handbook for designing problem-solving learning environments*. New York, NY: Routledge.

Luke, A. (2012). Critical literacy: Foundational notes. *Theory into Practice, 51*, 4–11.

Matters, G. (2006). The new basics: Good data, bad news, good policy making. *Queensland Teachers Union Professional Magazine*, October, 18–24.

The New London Group (1996). A pedagogy of multiliteracies: Designing social futures. *Harvard Educational Review, 66*, 60–92.

NRICH (2008). *Integrating rich tasks*. Retrieved March 28, 2016, from www.nrich.maths.org

Rustin, S. (2016). Think before you drink – about how to recycle your coffee cup. *The Guardian*. Retrieved March 16, 2016, from www.theguardian.com/commentisfree/2016/mar/16/takeaway-coffee-cups-recycle-environment-waste

Turner, S. (2013). *Teaching primary mathematics*. London, UK: SAGE Publications Ltd. Retrieved from www.londontoolkit.com/blog/eats/coffee-shop-chains-in-london/

7 | Changing times

Critical numeracy

Chapter 6 introduced critical literacy (New London Group, 1996) and posited the idea that a similar pedagogical approach could be adopted in mathematics. Just as critical literacy approaches "view language, texts, and their discourse structures as principal means for representing and reshaping possible worlds" (Luke, 2012, p. 6), a critical numeracy approach would present teachers with opportunities to engage pupils in reviewing mathematical structures and systems in order to interrogate possible worlds. At the very least, such an approach provides the raison d'être for encouraging pupils to engage in authentic investigations that, while not always solving problems, at least contribute to richer mental models of the phenomenon at their conclusion. Such approaches require an appreciation of the situated learning approach that Askew (2012) discusses when looking at the research undertaken by Lave (1988), who investigated how women used fractions in their everyday lives. She discovered that while the women had quite sophisticated and practical mental models of measuring fractional quantities of food for their diets they could not find answers to similar questions when presented with textbook examples. Lave (1988) argued that learning is far more context dependent, and Askew (2012) suggests her work challenges the idea of the transference of learning. I believe that such judgments may fail to take into account the richness of the mental models that individuals build over time to deal with phenomena in their environment.

I studied statistical analysis as part of an undergraduate business degree and was quite successful in completing the complex mathematics required for the course. Subsequently I have bought and sold property with the benefit of mortgages, travelled and migrated internationally and been able to negotiate currency exchange and all of the required mathematical calculations to judge relative costs and value when using a mental model of Australian dollars within a context of British pounds. I judge part of

105

my success in life by my ability to thrive economically (staying solvent can be viewed as thriving) and to even saving a little along the way. If someone was to give me a textbook example today of the type of calculations I so successfully completed for my business degree many years ago, I would be quite incapable of solving them. Why is that? I had competence and understanding then, I have transferred what knowledge was necessary for successful negotiation of my context now, yet I have not retained the sophisticated knowledge that I was so immersed in all that time ago because I don't use that knowledge for problems in my work or social life.

I believe that most adults, even those who profess to be poor at mathematics, generally have functional mental models sufficient for their success in everyday life. This proficiency can be challenged when they are confronted with their children bringing textbook examples of mathematics home or when someone asks them to write a mathematical operation down to solve a problem that is somewhat outside their usual realm of everyday life practice. In other words, we use 'rule of thumb' or heuristics regularly to solve the problems in our world, and these are mostly quite sophisticated and usually successful without having to justify a written answer to a third person. I agree with Askew (2012, p. 28) when he says that teachers have a "huge influence over learning but there are limits to that influence" particularly if we fail to take into account how children will actually use mathematics in their adult lives.

Fleury (2011) argues about how history as a subject taught by teachers helps prepare citizens for an active role in society, and a similar argument can be made for mathematics, just as Askew stated. Fleury (2011) highlighted the word *critical* in his discussion about history in which a learner's knowledge of the thinking process is necessary if they are to engage in dissent. He criticized the "well-intentioned promotion of a more critical, reflective and participatory citizenship being brought about by a systemic advocacy of topically framed standards" (Fleury, 2011, p. 80), which suggests that any effective inquiry does not have to fit a predetermined (often by someone else) form within a regimented curriculum constrained by testing. Similarly Freedman (2007, p. 467) agreed that if learners are to engage in learning through critical thinking then ideas from "multiple positions on . . . issues" must enter the classroom. The only way that such opportunities to explore ideas in a critical way can enter the classroom is through you, the teacher. When you, as a creative teacher, do bring criticality to your mathematical learning experiences you need to be prepared for the multiple interpretations that will follow due to the idiosyncratic mental models of your pupils.

Dewey's influence over education has been significant, and I believe his focus on the learner and how their wealth of individual experience can guide pedagogical design (Dewey, 1938) offers teachers an insight into the capacity of the learner to enact their own innovative and personalized strategies in the pursuit of solutions to challenging problems. Welsh and Murray (2003, p. 230) also offer the idea that being able to problematize an issue or phenomenon enables pupils to become "active knowledge producers instead of passive recipients". This idea of problematizing a phenomenon is not new, and earlier Dehler (1996) said that it enables intentional learning in which the individual is able to recall prior knowledge to which they can relate new ideas in order to reach and assess conclusions. I believe that it is this process of recall from richly secured mental models that enables individuals, such as the women in Lave's (1988) study, to interact successfully with their environment mathematically on a day-to-day basis even though such interactions could not be substantiated in a written form. They were, in effect, doing the maths rather than recording the maths. They were acting, and indeed thinking, numerically. There are many definitions of 'numeracy' or what it means to be numerate. I value the one used by the Education Department of Tasmania (1995, p. 5, cited in Commonwealth of Australia, 1997, p. 13) that says "to be numerate is to have and be able to use mathematical knowledge, understanding, skills, intuition and experience wherever they are needed in everyday life". This definition is of value because it refers to the 'use' of mathematics 'purposefully'. What does this discussion have to do with the title of the chapter? I posed a couple of key issues in the opening paragraphs which I will elucidate before presenting the next challenging task for learners in your classroom.

I argue that a critical numeracy approach enables pupils to develop the skills that are necessary for flourishing lives. It develops the ability to make useful decisions about everyday issues that involve some mathematical concepts. It applies a similar model to the Four Resource Model of Critical Literacy that Freebody and Luke (1990) designed to develop pupils' ability to ask questions about the meaning, validity and usefulness of texts that contain numerical information or concepts. The model they proposed has four processes: *De-coding* where concepts, terminology and mathematical ideas are explored; *Meaning making* where what the text is presenting and what is already known is critiqued; *Using,* which requires an interrogation of the purpose of the text, how it might be used and the possible impacts of its use to be done; and, *Analyzing* where judgments on the text's validity, logic, fairness, values and how it positions us are made (Freebody & Luke, 1990). The processes make matters that exist in the fabric of phenomena more visible and therefore more available for critique. A critical numeracy approach acknowledges that there are dangers for individuals where there is "autocratic control of information" and that there exists a "moral imperative of critique" (Luke, 2012, p. 5). Luke (2012, p. 5) explains that "human agency, self-determination, and freedom are put at risk" when open access and critique of information is closed down or controlled for any reason. He suggests that there are key curriculum questions for whose version of reality will be expressed in what is taught in schools just as there are key pedagogical questions about how it is taught.

A critical numeracy approach therefore requires the expression of mathematics and how it is selected, displayed, delivered and taught be interrogated to see if any of these processes contribute to social disenfranchisement of any individual rather than the social justice that each person is entitled to. It may sound like rhetoric, but it is a social imperative given the exploding use of confusion marketing (buy one get

Changing times

one free), misleading deals (you can borrow up to £500 now and not have to pay it back for 12 months) and jargon-filled contracts (read the fine print on any mobile phone contract) that consumers are increasingly exposed to in the modern world. The existence of comparison websites is sufficient reason to demonstrate the complexity that surrounds seemingly straightforward purchasing decisions that once were made about such matters as who was going to supply your electricity. The way that financial and numerical information is presented is designed, at times, to be misleading, and pupils require skill to understand such positioning in order to make decisions that will affect their lives. A critical numeracy approach enables pupils to make sense of the mathematical concepts in their lives through exploring multiple views often with the intention of using their new knowledge and understanding to create something useful and meaningful. It gives the mathematics we teach real purpose.

Problem posing

Problematization of issues or problem-posing tasks have been used by Mestre (2002) and Jonassen (2011) in order to probe pupils' understanding of concepts and if they could transfer this understanding to unique contexts. Mestre's (2002) tasks were in the context of a physics problem in which pupils were given a scenario and asked to construct a problem around it. These problems were often delivered in picture form, and pupils could use anything they had learned in the creation of their problem. Jonassen's (2011) variation, while still based in physics, required the pupils to read a statement that described a situation and then to add a question that would turn the situation into a problem that used specific principles rather than general knowledge as had Mestre's (2002). Jonassen (2011) continued this approach to explore the potential of using the models of problems that the pupils were creating to assess other learners' problem schemas that would work to keep the context of the work the pupils were engaged in fresh and context relevant. While I'm not proposing that teachers take the development of problem-posing tasks to that length, the proposition of offering something either in graphical form or an explanation for pupils to investigate offers a considerable opportunity to develop critical numeracy attitudes because it provides the raison d'être to challenge the orthodoxy of the phenomenon.

The following problem-posing task provides a significant opportunity for teachers to provide an investigation that is self-differentiating. Pupils can investigate to the depth and breadth of their own interests, and all levels will provide rich opportunities for practising the numerical, problem-solving and investigative skills that Turner (2013) saw as being essential for pupils to strengthen their mathematical knowledge. It is not a real problem and is unlikely to ever appear in our lifetimes. But its novelty

Changing times

provides an experience that investigates a phenomenon that is part of the fabric of our lives while offering many opportunities to challenge orthodox situations, practices and artifacts. So let's explore some problem space.

Problem posing: changing times

This activity poses the problem of the necessity of changing time to a 20-hour day rather than a 24-hour day. The actual amount of time in a day, in terms of minutes, would not change. But the move to a decimal equivalent time measure would bring societies in line with the move toward decimalization. It would be best suited for pupils 10 years of age and above, which would mean that in England and Wales they would be working on Key Stage 2 aspects of the national curriculum in mathematics (DfE, 2013). I would propose that they would be engaged in multiple strands of mathematics throughout this investigation, including measurement, statistics, fractions and the use of all operations. Table 7.1 presents the statutory and non-statutory requirements of the national curriculum of England and Wales (DfE, 2013) that pupils should be exposed to during this investigation for measurement, statistics and fractions.

Table 7.1 DfE (2013) outline of strands of the national curriculum covered in this activity

Strand	Statutory/ Non-statutory	Year Five	Year Six
Measurement	Statutory	Solve problems involving converting between units of time (p. 36)	Use, read, write and convert between standard units, converting measurements of time from a smaller unit of measure to a larger unit, and vice versa, using decimal notation to up to three decimal places (p. 43)
	Non-statutory	Use all four operations in problems involving time (p. 36)	They know approximate conversions and are able to tell if an answer is sensible (p. 43).

(Continued)

109

Table 7.1 (Continued)

Strand	Statutory/ Non-statutory	Year Five	Year Six
Statistics	Statutory	Complete, read and interpret information in tables, including timetables (p. 38)	
	Non-statutory	Pupils connect their work on coordinates and scales to their interpretation of time graphs. They begin to decide which representations of data are most appropriate and why (p. 38).	
Fractions	Statutory	Compare and order fractions whose denominators are all multiples of the same number Identify, name and write equivalent fractions of a given fraction, represented visually, including tenths and hundredths (p. 34)	Solve problems involving unequal sharing and grouping using knowledge of fractions and multiples (p. 42) Solve problems which require answers to be rounded to specified degrees of accuracy Recall and use equivalences between simple fractions, decimals and percentages, including in different contexts (p. 41)
	Non-statutory	Pupils should be taught throughout that percentages, decimals and fractions are different ways of expressing proportions. They extend their knowledge of fractions to thousandths and connect to decimals and measures (p. 34).	They practise calculations with simple fractions and decimal fraction equivalents to aid fluency, including listing equivalent fractions to identify fractions with common denominators (p. 41).

Changing times

I spent 3 hrs 45 min at the shop and took 1 hr 25 min to travel there and back. How long was I gone?

Hr	Min		Hr
3	45		3.45
1	25		1.25
4 hr	70 min	= 5 hr 10 min	4.70 hr

Figure 7.1 Adding time durations means using a different base

One of the most challenging concepts to teach young children is time. While learning how to tell the time is introduced in Year One, learning how to calculate time differences, durations and comparisons continue to be included in mathematics lessons throughout Primary school and indeed feature consistently in higher Key Stage schemes of work and assessment instruments. It is a challenging concept often fraught with misconceptions due, in part, to its base of computation being different to a decimal or base 10 system. The retention of such measures as 60 seconds in a minute and 60 minutes in an hour can be forgotten when calculations such as adding duration of times, shown in Figure 7.1, are being done: the reflex to resort to what is most frequently done when adding decimal numbers can often override the understanding that the base is different for time.

Enabling

The problem being posed to the children can be delivered by a couple of routes. One is to provide an image such as that shown in Figure 7.2 in which a clock with 10 hours has been created and pupils are expected to ask a question that fits with the implications embedded in the image. *What's wrong with this clock? What would need to change if we decimalized the hours in a day?*

The other way to pose the problem is to establish the context through a believable explanation of why moving to a 20-hour day is feasible – or even reasonable. Teachers working with younger pupils often use the pretext of a letter written by someone in authority, often the head teacher, to request that pupils respond to a problem or request. Or the context could be introduced with what happens when major changes occur in communities from around the world. Such changes have occurred in Australia with the change from pounds, shillings, pence to dollars or decimal currency in 1966, and in Sweden with the change to driving from the left-hand side of the road to the right-hand side on Sunday 3 September 1967 at 5 a.m. The day was referred to as Dagen H or H Day. H stands for Hogertrafik or right-hand traffic, which gives a clear indication of expected behaviour following the change. All traffic was stopped

Changing times

Figure 7.2 Clock showing 10 hours on the dial used to prompt the problem being posed

for one hour before hand when the signs were changed. A reduced speed limit was imposed until the change was complete a month later. After this Iceland changed in 1968, Nigeria in 1972, and Ghana in 1974. There are some videos available on the web, so demonstrating these major changes in countries can be shown to the pupils.

The UK also had a major change of currency on Decimal Day on 15 February 1971 when the nation moved to the decimalized pound. Until 1971 there were 20 shillings to a pound and 12 pence to a shilling, making 240 pence to a pound. After the change there were 100 pence to a pound, which is what many adults and indeed all children today would have ever known. The old currency was:

$1/3$ = 80 pence said as 6 shilling and 8 pence or 6/8

$1/4$ = 60 pence said as 5 shillings

$1/5$ = 48 pence said as 4 shillings

$1/6$ = 40 pence said as 3 shillings and 4 pence or 3/4

It might be useful to have some examples of the money available to show the children what it looked like and, perhaps, to do some calculations on equivalent values today. What these changes demonstrate is that great changes to the fabric of our lives can be made and that when they do, systems and artifacts have to change as well. Exploring some of those necessary changes in 1971 would demonstrate how embedded in our culture many mathematical artifacts are.

Engaging

Explaining

However you choose to introduce the *need* to change the time, a session in which the concept is brainstormed and explored allows the first critical numeracy step of de-coding (Freebody & Luke, 1990) in which the concepts of time including processes, terminology and systems, are explored and explained. Many of the *what* questions associated with *explaining* should be asked by the pupils and by the teacher and important information recorded in some way as a repository of knowledge for the pupils to access during their investigation. Pupils in the class can be recorders of the information, because having this responsibility gives them rich experience of a community role.

Most of the discussion in the first session would revolve around what pupils know about:

- Measures of time (seconds, minutes, hours, days, weeks)
- Systems of time (timetables, automated clocks, durations of phenomena)
- Artifacts of time (clocks – digital and analogue)

Once a critique of the current state has been explored through questions, pupils will be required to make decisions as to what they would need to plan for to implement the change by a certain date. This would involve making predictions about the next steps and possible outcomes as well as using the *meaning-making* process of Freebody and Luke's (1990) Four Resource Model. It would be useful at this point if the pupils were working in groups and to select one aspect of the change that they would be responsible for designing and developing. The options for the decision-making aspect of this step would depend on the experiences and mental models of the pupils, but as a guide, you would be looking for ideas around:

- Clock design (now need 10 rather than 12 digits and spaces, so the best shapes for this need to be explored)
- Timetable changes (now have 20 hours in the day – calculations needed to plan new durations of lessons, movies, bus journeys or any other timetable that is relevant to children's lives)

The activity becomes self-differentiating because the pupils can enter the investigation at a point that is challenging but comfortable for them. It will also be necessary to alert the class to how many aspects of the change you will be requiring them to consider. While some children will be energized to grapple with complex system changes (international timelines or flight schedules) some will be able to deal with increasing levels of difficulty through a stepped approach.

Changing times

Examining

Predicting

The predicting step would require pupils to use what they already know to make predictions on what else they need to explore or change. They might ask questions such
as *How can I use what I know to design a particular aspect of the change?* A table of
the information that is relevant for the change is shown in Table 7.2 and would be a
useful starting point for all pupils to develop.

One of the conceptual elements of the investigation that pupils need to grasp is
that there will not be any more or less time in the day: the structure of the hour will
be changing so that any artifact or system dependent on the concept of the hour will
need to change. You would be working to ensure that the pupils arrive at this understanding rather than telling them.

Other questions that will be of use to prompt pupils' investigations in either rede-
signing clock faces or the systems dependent on hourly time are:

Clock design

> *What do you think the result will be if you stay with a circular clock face?*
>
> *What might be another shape that will make a suitable clock face for 10 hours?*

Timetable system design

> *What do you think you need to change in the timetable to show the new hour at
> 72 minutes?*
>
> *What other things might you need to consider so the commuters still have the
> same schedules to catch a train? (If two trains arrive every hour [with 60 min-
> utes] how often should they come in the new hour to deliver the same service?)*

Table 7.2 Time changes required for the investigation

	Existing	Proposed
Hours in day	24	20
Minutes in day	1,440	1,440
Seconds in day	86,400	86,400
Minutes in hour	60	72
Seconds in hour	3,600	4,320
Seconds in minute	60	60

Other possible systems

> *What might happen to speed cameras on the roads when the clocks change?*
>
> *What happens to people's pay scales when the clocks change?*

These system changes are quite complex calculations, but they do allow pupils who are eager for a challenge to start applying their understanding of fractions and proportion in a real-life investigation. The fractions that pupils will need to be explore include:

½ hour   30 v 36 min
¼ hour   15 v 18 min
¾ hour   45 v 54 min

These changes might have implications for other changes, and it is important to not feel any trepidation about what the pupils might come up with. The idiosyncratic nature of their mental models because of the diversity of their ethnic, social and familial experiences will provide a rich source of ideas, most of which you may not have considered. There may even be some cultural and religious aspects, such as regular prayer, that become visible due to the reliance on an hourly or daily schedule. These can be handled with dexterity by most teachers by using an ecopedagogical experience of education (Kahn, 2010) that Freedman (2007, p. 467) says is important so that teachers can present multiple positions on "salient public issues and train students in a method of analyzing these positions" so as to develop those critical thinking skills that the curriculum (DfE, 2013) has embedded in its aims. As pupils progress through their investigation, they will be constantly diagnosing their position and their use and understanding of knowledge.

Evaluating

Diagnosing

Jonassen (2011) sees diagnosing as a process similar to pattern recognition, and this would be quite a useful consideration when evaluating what is occurring in this investigation as pupils progress. At some point they would see replication of pattern to be useful for moving their artifacts forward particularly with the new regularity of the timings necessary for timetables and other schedules dependent on the segmenting of the day into hours. What you would expect to see at this stage of the investigation is that pupils will have applied their new understandings of time to design either a new artifact or system element (timetable or schedule). Most of the prompts that you would use at this stage would be about testing the outcomes for plausibility and usability.

If we looked at Freebody and Luke's (1990) model the questions would also prompt the pupils to enact the *Using* process, in which they would need to consider the possible applications of the artifacts they have designed.

Clock design

> *Why did you choose to use a circle for the design and what did it mean you had to do differently?*
>
> *Why did the triangle not work?*
>
> *Why did the pentagon work well for a 10/20 hour clock?*
>
> *Have you considered every possible shape for a clock face?*

Timetable system design

> *Why did your timetable for buses work?*
>
> *Why did your timetable for buses not work? Did you consider using a table to compare the differences between the new times and the old times? Why might that be a reasonable process?*
>
> *Why might you try something else?*

Other possible systems

> *Why would our speeds have to change before you could change the cameras?*
>
> *Why might people feel they are receiving less in their pay if the clocks change?*
>
> *Why might you be able to talk on the phone to your friends for longer with decimal time?*

Once pupils have completed one aspect of the investigation, they can move on to another aspect, and this is probable given the nature of the investigation. Layers of complexity are revealed as pupils uncover the interconnectedness of systems. Of course they would not be expected to be familiar with complex, adult systems such as pay rates. However, a teacher who is willing to allow the knowledge development in their classroom to have the emancipatory potential that Welsh and Dehler (2001) feel is necessary for pupils to develop the capacity to act on what they are learning would encourage pupils to pursue whatever investigation they thought was relevant. How you, as a teacher, manage the investigations is dependent on many organizational issues and constraints. But ensuring that all pupils successfully complete at least one line of investigation will ensure that the final communication and analysis of ideas is of benefit to all.

Communicating

What did you learn in school today? On the final day of the investigations pupils should be provided with an opportunity to display and share what they have found in the format most suitable for your context. This might be in static displays that are 'manned', ready for visitors to view and ask questions. Or you might prefer each group to present their results in a more formal oral presentation. Whatever form it takes, inviting outside-the-classroom guests is beneficial for the pupils because it means that they have an audience for their learning. Such formal opportunities also enable Freebody and Luke's (1990) final process, Analyzing, to be done. Here, questions such as the following can be asked to judge the efficacy of the change of time.

> *Are the mathematical concepts used appropriately in the artifact?*
>
> *Has the artifact been created using a reasonable design?*
>
> *Are there any unfair assumptions in the artifact?*
>
> *Has the change been shown correctly and truly in the artifact?*

The quality and depth of the interrogation at this stage would need to rely on the quality of the criticality you have exposed your pupils to throughout the investigation, because it would be unfair to thrust new questions onto pupils at this point. However, the evaluation and communication should not be tokenistic either. If pupils have invested a considerable amount of thought and effort in their design, then due consideration of its relevance, authenticity and accountability should be made. Jonassen (2011, p. 163) suggests that "learning is driven by acceptance of a meaningful goal", so to make the activity in Changing Times meaningful the outcomes should be judged, primarily, in terms of the relevance the artifact will have to their lives.

Moving forward

Problems really are everywhere, so the development of a problem such as the need to change the time may be seen as a step into fairyland or make-believe. However, the existence of a system of time that we do have and that we teach to children is rarely, if ever, challenged by rational debate. I remember when I lived in Queensland, Australia, and we had two referenda to decide whether or not we, as a state, would move our clocks forward and backward throughout the year as other states did when moving into and out of the summer months. The debate leading to the vote became irrational when people started phoning chat lines on the radio to complain that *"if we have more daylight then the curtains will fade"* or *"the cows won't know when to come in for milking"*. Needless to say Queensland doesn't move their clocks around, and this unwillingness to alter nature has as many arguments for and against as does the day have hours. What the debate did engender was an interrogation of a system that is part of the fabric of people's lives, and therefore it was of relevance and value regardless of the outcome. What was also necessary for people to even enter the debate was to have a reasonable understanding or knowledge of the concepts and value of time; they needed to be numerate. What this activity, Changing Times, offers for your class is an opportunity to apply the knowledge they have been developing throughout their Primary school years so as to develop richer and more robust mental models of time.

References

Askew, M. (2012). *Transforming primary mathematics.* Oxon, UK: Routledge.

Commonwealth of Australia (1997). *Numeracy = everyone's business: The report of the Numeracy Education Development Strategy Conference May 1997.* Adelaide, SA: Australian Association of Mathematics Teachers Inc.

Dehler, G. E. (1996). Management education as intentional learning: A knowledge-transforming approach to written composition. *Journal of Management Education, 20*(2), 221–235.

Department for Education (2013). *The national curriculum for England and Wales.* London, UK: DfE.

Dewey, J. (1938). *Experience and education.* New York, NY: Palgrave Macmillan.

Fleury, S. (2011). Playing with fire, or the stuffing of dead animals: Freire, Dewey, and the dilemma of social studies reform. *Educational Studies, 47,* 71–91.

Freebody, P., & Luke, A. (1990). Literacies programs: Debates and demands in cultural context. *Prospect: An Australian Journal of TESOL, 5*(3), 7–16.

Freedman, E. B. (2007). Is teaching for social justice undemocratic? *Harvard Educational Review, 77,* 443–473.

Jonassen, D. H. (2011). *Learning to solve problems: A handbook for designing problem-solving learning environments.* New York, NY: Routledge.

Kahn, R. (2010). *Critical pedagogy, ecoliteracy and planetary crisis: The ecopedagogy movement.* New York, NY: Peter Lang.

Lave, J. (1988). *Cognition in practice: Mind, mathematics and culture in everyday life.* Cambridge: Cambridge University Press.

Luke, A. (2012). Critical literacy: Foundational notes. *Theory into Practice, 51,* 4–11.

Mestre, J. (2002). Probing adults' conceptual understanding and transfer of learning via problem posing. *Journal of Applied Developmental Psychology, 23*(1), 9–50.

New London Group (1996). A pedagogy of multiliteracies: Designing social futures. *Harvard Educational Review, 66,* 60–92.

Turner, S. (2013). *Teaching primary mathematics.* London, UK: SAGE Publications Ltd.

Welsh, M. A., & Dehler, G. E. (2001). *Paradigm, praxis and paradox in the analysis of organization change: The generative nature of control.* Proceedings of the 2nd International Critical Management Studies Conference, Manchester, UK.

Welsh, M. A., & Murray, D. L. (2003). The ecollaborative: Teaching sustainability through critical pedagogy. *Journal of Management Education, 27*(2), 220–235.

8 Problem solving and investigating

Further ideas

This final chapter returns to the key points raised throughout this text about teaching and learning through mathematical problem solving and investigations: an understanding of the different ways that individuals think, knowledge of the diverse ways that teachers can present learning opportunities and an appreciation of the impact such approaches have on how individual students learn mathematics is key to effective teaching and learning through problem solving in mathematics. This chapter presents a summary of these aspects to demonstrate how you can embrace problem solving and investigating in your classroom. We aim to encourage you to think about how you will engage the students in challenging (and life-changing?) activities in mathematics.

Some further exploration of ideas will help illuminate the paths that teachers may decide to take in their classroom as they work with children to develop mathematical competency and confidence. We would agree, as a profession, that it is the teacher's responsibility to establish an environment that offers each and every child the opportunity to flourish mathematically. One way that teachers may be abrogating this responsibility is through the reliance on schemes of work that places the responsibility on someone else, in a different context and with a different purpose, to establish the most suitable mathematical learning programme for the students in their class. Schemes are convenient, and many have been thoroughly prepared for the 'busy' teacher who may wish to have a systematic way of 'delivering' the curriculum particularly if they are in a multi-form entry school. There are many head teachers who choose such an approach in order to have continuity of vocabulary, approaches, lesson structure and assessment design across their schools. But the teachers who

121

Problem solving and investigating

work with the students and each other on a daily basis can better develop a schematic approach in the school itself. The decision is often time based (efficiency) rather than quality based (effectiveness).

Another way that teachers may inadvertently relinquish their responsibility is to encourage students to establish SMART targets in mathematics particularly at the end of a unit of work, strand or term. An increasing number of adjectives can be attributed to the acronym 'SMART', which indicates that individuals or groups find the letters themselves problematic. Some we have encountered include:

S: specific, significant, stretching;
M: measurable, meaningful, motivational;
A: agreed, acceptable, action oriented;
R: realistic, relevant, reasonable; and,
T: time-based, tangible, trackable.

Take your pick! It is clear that too many new words now entering this acronym's lexicon demonstrates how unlikely such an approach will be to lead to success for all. Instead, if faced with the unenviable task of creating a SMART target, students (and indeed their teachers!) should be asking questions that mirror the critical numeracy approach discussed in Chapter 6 such as:

Significant for whom?

Why must my work toward this target be measurable?

Who will be measuring it using which instrument?

Agreed? Who is in agreement? How am I being positioned to agree with such targets/measures/learning?

If I don't reach the 'agreed' place in the 'agreed' time is my learning of less value? Do I stop and make another SMART target?

Such prompts would empower a learner far more than the establishment of some acronym which attempts to pass the responsibility for learning from the teacher to the learner (or, at a higher level, from the organization to the teacher). Strauss (2001) was right when he explained that the way many teachers understand how children learn (part of their folk psychology) influences the way that they teach. But increasingly people outside the classroom are making decisions about what is actually taught in the classroom and how it is taught. Strauss was interested in how teachers taught, and he used the mental model construct as the heuristic. We've discussed mental models quite extensively in the earlier chapters, but to remind you, mental models allow individuals to understand their world and to allow them to make predictions when operating in different domains.

122

Mental models of children's minds and learning

I used the analogy of trying to find a light switch to enter a strange, darkened room to demonstrate how an individual will use past experiences, different procedural and propositional knowledge in order to solve a problem. Strauss (2001) used Norman's (1983) explanation of mental models to summarize how he believes teachers use mental models in terms of children's minds and how they learn. He said,

1. people's mental models reflect their beliefs about children's minds and learning;
2. there is a correspondence between parameters and states of the mental model and the aspects and states of children's minds and learning; and
3. the mental model has predictive power in that it allows people to understand and anticipate the behavior of children's minds and how learning takes place in them (Strauss, 2001, p. 225).

The work that Strauss (2001) did in linking Mental Model Theory directly to how teachers work with children in a learning environment (that is how they teach them) relied on a taxonomy of teacher knowledge proposed by Shulman (1986) and Wilson, Shulman and Richert (1987) which included pedagogical content knowledge otherwise known as PCK. PCK is used to capture the broad and deep knowledge that teachers have about how to teach subject matter to children and includes the teachers' considerations of such things as concepts, skills, preconceptions and misconceptions. Strauss (2001) called this knowledge of children's minds and how they work *folk psychology* and used the term *folk pedagogy* to define the role of instruction in developing and encouraging the learning. Strauss's (2001) work is important because it challenges some assumptions about the impact that a teacher's subject matter knowledge (SMK) has on the way that they teach. This argument about subject matter knowledge and pedagogical content knowledge is particularly relevant in mathematics, where Williams (2008) was particularly concerned with Primary teachers' competence and confidence to teach a subject that is at best confusing and at worst debilitating if simple procedures are not understood. While a focus on developing strong mathematical subject knowledge is integral, we believe, to rich teaching and learning, Strauss (2001) found that it was a teacher's mental model of children's mind and learning (their folk psychology) that was the main determiner of *how* they will teach (their folk pedagogy); a teacher's SMK might determine *what* they teach but will not determine *how* they teach. In other words, Strauss (2001) concluded that a teacher's SMK is subordinate to their mental models of children's mind and learning.

What are the implications of such views, and are they relevant to the ways a teacher will engage children in problem solving and investigations in mathematics? Chapter 3 discussed the creative aspects of mathematics and how ensuring learning tasks included flexibility of thinking that they could lead to new lines of investigation for students to explore (Haylock, 2010). Time is a key component of a stimulating mathematics-learning environment, and Askew (2012) is right to challenge the orthodoxy of trying to package learning into a lesson rather than leaving room for unresolved problems to be pondered a little longer. What can be clearly seen as causing concern for teachers, particularly in England and Wales as they work through the national curriculum in mathematics (DfE, 2013), is the lack of a distinct strand for problem solving and the light touch provided in guidance within statutory requirements.

There is little time in teacher education to explore a beginning teacher's mental model of children's minds and learning (Strauss, 2001) let alone how they will endeavour to develop rich physical and intellectual arenas in the classroom for children to develop problem-solving and investigative skills and knowledge. We would argue for a well-educated teaching population; Master's study engages teachers in the exploration of the ontological and epistemological beliefs and mental models necessary for productive reflection during teaching. In the meantime, we can support more immediately ways that teachers who may be unable to undertake further study develop a greater understanding of how to introduce and support students through closed and open inquiries in mathematics. Providing such scaffolds of how to present such challenging building blocks of investigating mathematical structures can enable teachers and allow them to build the confidence and competence (understanding) to teach mathematics well.

Being neat and messy at the same time!

We've presented various activities in the preceding chapters that are closed and open. To remind you:

CLOSED:
Problems start messy, and the problem-solving process enables them to become neat.

OPEN:
Investigations start neat, and the problem-solving process enables them to become messy.

One of the questions is can an inquiry change and be both? We have an example.

Problem posed to children:
On an abacus 3 beads are placed on hundreds, tens and ones 'rods' (positions). How many different numbers can be made?

The teacher would encourage the students (Year Three children could work with this activity either individually, in pairs or fours) to use beads, column headings on large pieces of paper or moving lists of numbers on cards to record what they find. Some

Problem solving and investigating

students will use a random approach, but what teachers who have a focus on how children's minds work (Strauss, 2001) would start to notice is that some will develop a systematic way of showing and recording what they find. If a teacher *shows* how to record the answer they are removing the opportunity for children to construct their own understanding through discovery. Opportunities for sharing the task increase the likelihood that someone in the pair/group will identify a way of recording the answers so that none are missed. The list below is a logical one starting at the largest number:

```
H T O
3 0 0

2 1 0
2 0 1

1 2 0
1 1 1
1 0 2

0 3 0
0 2 1
0 1 2
0 0 3
```

So the solutions that children find should add up to 10 numbers in all. Mini plenary sessions, or indeed an end-of-class plenary session, would enable children to compare their results to those of others, and this opportunity for discussion is important because it encourages children to talk about their processes and results thereby empowering all children to develop richer mental models of such a systematic, logical process for problem solving.

However, rather than looking at the *total number of* distinctive digits found, asking students to structure their results according to the number of digits in the *hundreds* column enables them to see a pattern emerge:

```
              H T O
1    {        3 0 0

2    {        2 1 0
     {        2 0 1

3    {        1 2 0
     {        1 1 1
     {        1 0 2
```

Problem solving and investigating

$$
4 \quad \left\{ \begin{array}{ccc} 0 & 3 & 0 \\ 0 & 2 & 1 \\ 0 & 1 & 2 \\ 0 & 0 & 3 \end{array} \right.
$$

As shown, a pattern of 1, 2, 3, 4 numbers in each successive group can be identified and explains the total of 10 as addition of numbers: $1 + 2 + 3 + 4 = 10$ and this is a triangular number. Such a deviation in the problem-solving activity invites an additional related question: Is there a similar relationship between the numbers it is possible to make if other numbers of beads are used? The identification of such a relationship and a related or follow up question could transform the **closed** problem into an **investigation**.

The **neat** closed solution could become a small part of a much larger *messy* exploration with examples shown in what follows:

1 bead

H T O
1 0 0

0 1 0
0 0 1

$1 + 2 = 3$

2 beads

H T O
2 0 0

1 1 0
1 0 1

0 2 0
0 1 1
0 0 2

$1 + 2 + 3 = 6$

At four beads make a prediction based on what has come before with 1, 2 and 3 beads.

H T O
4 0 0

3 1 0
3 0 1

Problem solving and investigating

```
2  2  0
2  1  1
2  0  1

1  3  0
1  2  1
1  1  2
1  0  3

0  4  0
0  3  1
0  2  2
0  1  3
0  0  4
```

$1 + 2 + 3 + 4 + 5 = 15$

And so on . . .

So what we have discovered is that the middle part of the activity is problem solving in which the process is messy but there is only one answer. The teacher's skill is to guide the children to develop their own skills to open up the activity so that it becomes an investigation with infinite explanations and solutions. A similar activity was discussed in Chapter 4 with number strings, but in this example we have used a simple activity to demonstrate how approaches to problem solving can be both closed and open and to understand that once one solution is found it does not have to signify a *neat ending* to the activity. Indeed, challenging ourselves as teachers and the children in our class as students to look at problems in a multitude of ways opens up our minds to significant opportunities to find the relationships in mathematics that Skemp (1976/2006) continued to promote in seeking relational learning. We all become learners, teachers and students alike, and in the process develop richer mental models of ourselves as capable problem solvers.

In closing

We hope that this exploration of problem solving and investigating in Primary mathematics has challenged you to gain greater understanding of the ways in which individuals think and how you, as a teacher, can design learning activities that enable children to become successful problem solvers and investigators. We have based the contents on both research and experience in the belief that it is increasingly necessary for teachers to have not only a rich palette of mathematical investigations available for their students but to also have an understanding of how to act during them so that children experience the opportunities to *construct* their own understandings rather than being led to a definitive answer. Life is not neat, and we are doing a disservice to our students if we only prepare them to find one answer: they will enter many different darkened rooms in their lives, and we are beholden to prepare them to find the light switch most suitable to light the way.

References

Askew, M. (2012). *Transforming primary mathematics*. Oxon, UK: Routledge.

Department for Education (2013). *The national curriculum for England and Wales*. London, UK: DfE.

Haylock, D. (2010). *Mathematics explained for primary teachers* (4th ed.). London, UK: SAGE Publications Ltd.

Norman, D. A. (1983). Some observations on mental models. In D. Gentner & A. L. Stevens (Eds.), *Mental models* (pp. 7–14). Hillsdale, NJ: Lawrence Erlbaum.

Shulman, L. S. (1986). Those who understand: Knowledge growth in teaching. *Educational Researcher, 15*, 4–14.

Skemp, R. (1976/2006). Relational understanding and instrumental understanding. *Mathematics Teaching in the Middle School, 12*(2), 88–95. Originally published in Mathematics Teaching.

Strauss, S. (2001). Folk psychology, folk pedagogy, and their relations to subject-matter knowledge. In B. Torff & R. J. Sternberg (Eds.), *Understanding and teaching the intuitive mind: Student and teacher learning*. Mahwah, NJ: Lawrence Erlbaum.

Williams, P. (2008). *Independent review of mathematics teaching in early years settings and primary schools*. Final Report. London, UK: Department for Children, Schools and Families.

Wilson, S. M., Shulman, L. S., & Richert, A. E. (1987). "150 different ways" of knowing: Representations of knowledge in teaching. In J. Calderhead (Ed.), *Exploring teachers' thinking* (pp. 104–124). London, UK: Cassell Education.

Appendix 1
Assessment strategy for PGCE student teachers

The assignment has two parts:

Part 1: mathematical investigation – *personal mathematical endeavour and critical reflection*

(*equivalent to 1,200 words*).

This will be a 'sketchbook' which documents your exploration (comprising a maximum of 12 A4 pages of mathematical endeavour and 1 page of critical reflection); highlighting and explaining both your mathematical achievements (what you learned) and learning process (how you learned).

(a) You will be expected to explore different lines of inquiry in sufficient depth to provide a personal challenge by:

- Making decisions – posing questions to pursue, selecting strategies and generating examples in order to explore numerical strategies and relationships;
- Communicating your results – organizing and presenting results creatively and coherently;
- Analyzing and explaining your discoveries – identifying, describing and justifying patterns and mathematical relationships in relation to number strategies, algebra, diagrams and models.

Appendix 1

Your ideas and thinking should be creatively displayed

Developing discoveries and understanding should be demonstrated and documented (using lists, diagrams, pictures, number lines, grids, charts, graphs, calculations, photographs, etc.)

– Ongoing analysis of your 'learning journey' should be tracked and reconstructed (through informal notes and comments, possibly employing headlines, Post-it notes, stickers and coloured pens).

(b) You will be expected to critically reflect on your mathematical discoveries and learning process by:

- Experiencing different ways of learning – initially working independently and then in pairs or small groups, scrutinizing your own and your peers' mathematical endeavours;
- Creating 'headlines' that structure and highlight your personal learning process – reflecting on your experiences and making annotations to your work, which track and explain your personal learning journey,
- Using a maximum of three stickers to identify key mathematical discoveries – highlighting and explaining how your mathematical understanding, thinking and/or appreciation have developed;
- Summarizing your learning process – identifying and explaining significant factors which influenced, supported and enabled you to extend your mathematical understanding, thinking skills and attitude to and appreciation of mathematics.

Your learning process should be summarized *(using approximately 250 words of typewritten prose and possibly diagrams) in order to highlight and explain both your mathematical achievements (what you learned) and learning process (how you learned).*

Assignment requirements and assessment

Both parts of the assignment must be passed in order to reach the course requirements. Tutors will assess:

Part 1: the quality of your informed analytical or creative insights into the identification of personal mathematical development (in relation to mathematical understanding, thinking skills, attitudes towards and appreciation of mathematics), as well as your demonstration of your understanding of mathematical structures and strategies.

Appendix 2
4R approach to collaboration

Society expects that when students leave formal schooling they not only have the academic competence to participate in life beyond the classroom but that they also have the interpersonal skills to make a sound contribution to that life. Employers, universities, colleges and recreational clubs are consistent in their interest in how an individual can *'work with others'*, *'be a team player'* or *'have good interpersonal skills'*. Learning to work effectively with others does not happen automatically for many learners. Anyone who has joined a committee, team or club would have experienced the range of 'types' that make up such social constructs. Indeed, each of us has a tendency to agree, disagree, dominate or submit to the demands of others. Sometimes our ignorance is to blame for poor behaviour in groups: we can be ignorant of the role that someone else is fulfilling or ignorant of our own strengths and weaknesses.

This approach to collaborative or cooperative group work was developed in Australian Primary classrooms, where I worked with children aged 10 years and above. The approach is simple enough to be introduced to learners as soon as they are able to read. A talented Early Years teacher could, I imagine, use it with learners who are yet to read! I was eager to have a method of 'educating' children to work together to produce one artifact. It needed to be simple, have clear boundaries and be memorable: it needed to be simply designed and effective. I believe that a group of four is most effective in the Primary school setting. There is a raft of research on optimal group size, which you may find useful to read, and you may have, already, your own preference. I found that a group of four enables each role to be a meaningful contribution while allowing for children to sit around a reasonably sized table. If a group member is absent it is also easy to double up a role and not lose the efficacy of the approach.

Appendix 2

Roles of the 4R Approach

Retriever	Reader
Leaves the workspace of the group to collect all materials relevant for the task. Having one person moving about reduces class congestion at the beginning of the session. If more materials are required during the activity, the rest of the group can continue working, thereby reducing opportunities for 'off-task' behaviour. Reprimands should be agreed if anyone other than the Retriever leaves the group during activity time. The retriever is also responsible for returning unused resources but is not solely responsible for tidying the workspace: the whole group is responsible for leaving a tidy workspace.	Reads the requirements of the task and any other resources necessary for the task to be started and completed. The reader is responsible for bringing the group back to focus if they go 'off task' during the activity. The reader is not solely responsible for interpreting the instructions, but they have to manage the delivery of them to all group members.
Recorder	**Responder**
Is responsible for ensuring that the one artifact, regardless of what it is, is prepared for sharing at the end of the activity. They are not solely responsible for contributing to its completion: all members of the group can contribute in some way. But it is their responsibility to delegate tasks and ensure the artifact is in a complete state at the end of the task.	Presents the final product or artifact to the rest of the class. They can either stand at the group table or move to the front of the class to share the result of the group effort. They may have recorded on paper what they will say or be able to describe it off the cuff. But they should have worked with the reader to ensure that they are able to respond to all criteria to demonstrate that the artifact is complete and meets the requirements of the task.

The roles are very clear and should be discussed with the learners so that they have no doubt as to the responsibilities for each. Accurate record keeping by the teacher in the beginning stages of use with learners is also essential to ensure that each child has the opportunity to experience each role so as to gain both an understanding of what they and the others in the group should be doing when working with others and the roles they feel most comfortable and proficient doing. Some children will find it quite difficult to do only one role, so surveillance and intervention may be necessary in the early stages to ensure that these individuals learn the boundaries.

132

Appendix 2

Assuring them that they will have a chance to do each role will encourage them to try each one and think about which they prefer and why.

Part of the activity's plenary sessions, particularly when you are introducing the approach, should be a discussion of the roles. It is an important part of the learning process that children begin to understand that we are all individuals and have differing mental models of phenomena. Tolerance of others comes from education and knowledge of self, so encouraging discussion about why we prefer different roles will begin the discussion about being an individual but being able to work well with others.

Suggestions for use of the 4R approach

In the first uses of the approach, try to give a 10-minute activity with minimal resources so that each learner has the opportunity to try a role, work with others who are in role and complete an artifact in a set period of time. Setting the time period for the activity is essential because it puts pressure on the group to make decisions and complete the artifact. Most of what individuals do for work or for pleasure has a time period allocated to it, so using a timed approach prepares learners to use time efficiently and effectively. They will also see the outcome of not doing so, which is also an integral aspect of learning.

Some of the areas of mathematics that lend themselves well to this approach are the creation of any artifact in geometry, statistics or algebra. You may also use it to solve some problems that are numerical. Keeping the task short in the first round of sessions so that all children have the chance to do each role will expose them to those roles but limit any disenfranchisement they may have to a short period of time. Extending the period of the activity after they have a working knowledge of the roles allows them to better explore their mental model of each, thereby gaining rich metacognitive understanding. Once you have done a couple of rounds (four activities per round to account for each individual doing each role), I would suggest that the groups themselves start to record who is doing which role. I would hesitate to leave it open for choice: some children will want to do only one role, and that will limit the functionality of the group. There may also be a clash of individuals who wish to do the same role, so ensuring they rotate through the roles will keep the approach more diplomatic and enable each child to develop the skills and understandings they need to be functional collaborators.

Good luck!

133

Appendix 3
Teacher's notes for squaring up to the problem

Note: the area for all of these shapes is 36cm²
Shapes that best meet all criteria are shaded.

Shape	Name	Tessellate?	Lines of symmetry	Order of rotational symmetry	Matching edge	Perimeter (cm to 1dp)
	Square	Yes	4	4	Diagonal or vertical	24
Made from a diagonal cut (two triangles)						
	Parallelogram	Yes	0	2	6cm side	29
	Isosceles Triangle	Yes	1	1	6cm side	29
Made from a vertical cut (two rectangles)						
	Long Rectangle	Yes	2	2	3cm	30
	T	Yes	1	0	3cm alongside of 6cm	30
	L	Yes	0	0	3cm alongside of 6cm	30

135

Shape	Name	Tessellate?	Lines of symmetry	Order of rotational symmetry	Matching edge	Perimeter (cm to 1dp)
Made from a diagonal cut 1cm from corners						
	Isosceles trapezium	Yes	1	1	6cm side	27.6
	Parallelogram	Yes	0	2	6cm side	27.6
	Convex Pentagon	No	1	1	5cm	29.6
	Concave Pentagon	No	1	1	1cm	37.6
	Hexagon (Bow)	No	0	2	1cm	37.6
	Hexagon (Pin)	No	0	1	5cm	29.6
	Concave Hexagon	No	1	1	Diagonal	24
Made from a diagonal cut 2cm from the corners						
	Isosceles Trapezium	Yes	1	1	6cm side	26.4
	Parallelogram	Yes	0	2	6cm side	26.4
	Convex Pentagon	No	1	1	5cm	28.4
	Concave Pentagon	No	1	1	1cm	36.4
	Hexagon (Bow)	No	0	2	1cm	36.4
	Hexagon (Pin)	No	0	2	1cm	36.4
	Concave Hexagon	No	1	1	Diagonal	24

Index

ability: grouping 13–14; mixed 20, 76; setting 13
accommodation 5
addition *see* operations
analogous structures 29
analogy 5, 9, 29, 123
argument 28, 42, 98, 106, 118, 123
assimilation 5, 25
attitudes 21, 28, 36, 63, 66, 92, 101, 108, 130
authentic: education 36; learning experiences 65; tasks 102, 105
autonomy 27, 102

behavior: disruptive 26–27, 131–132; individual 6, 27; normative 84; student 6, 27, 91
belief 6, 23, 28, 62, 123–124, 127; idiosyncratic 12; mistaken 15; new 24; shared 1
bimodal 30, 35

challenges 1, 2, 33, 45, 49, 69; design 76
chocolate 7, 95
cognitive: awareness 62; behavior 6; blisters 9, 28, 48; disequilibrium 36; functions 6; interactions 23, 34; processes 36; representation 11, 14; science 7; structures 6, 7, 9, 24, 30; theory 34
collaboration 12–13, 20, 51, 131
concept maps 13, 29–30
connectionism 23, 35
connectionist approach 7, 29–30, 62

creative: activity 12; approaches 41; aspects 123; insights 66, 130; investigations 73; soup 12; teacher 106; thinking 57
creativity 51, 79
critique 20, 29, 91, 94, 107, 113
curiosity 45, 101
curriculum: design & technology 32, 93; England & Wales 2, 8, 19, 21, 30, 42, 48, 62, 73, 78, 83, 86, 93, 95, 98, 109; mathematics 11, 13, 42, 44, 46, 49, 56, 64–65, 79, 90–91, 96, 124

decode 11
design 11, 51, 76, 80–82, 86, 92–93, 106, 113–117, 121; briefs 83
diagrams 9, 13, 29, 30, 47, 52–53, 69, 72, 78, 83, 129–130
discourse 11, 20, 28, 35–36, 105
disequilibrium 13, 26, 36, 76
division *see* operations

education: authentic 36; co-intentional 36; Queensland 89; teacher 124
experts 14–15, 30, 35

fluency 30

IDEAL 44, 50
inference 11, 28
inquiry 10, 14, 21, 25, 30, 37, 43, 51–52, 66, 82, 93, 106, 124; mathematical 9, 42
interrogation 107, 117–118; reflective 36

Index

knowledge: conceptual 14, 22, 69, 78; construction of 57; domain 48; individual 25; mathematical 43, 73, 77, 79, 107–108; new 6, 13, 19, 26, 28, 36, 90, 108; pedagogic content 123; procedural 9, 14, 22, 30, 69, 78, 123; propositional 6–7, 9, 14, 22, 30, 69, 78, 123; relational 95; retention of 42; storage of 8, 25, 26, 35; subject matter 123; tacit 13; teacher 123; types 7, 12, 92; variety 6

language: acquisition 24; appropriate 81; body 29; comprehension 10–11; mathematical 42, 98
learning: environment 29, 61, 64, 91, 123; learner-centred 8; material 2; mathematical 2, 41–42, 44, 106, 121, 124; problem-centred 8, 10; process of 23, 32, 66; relational 127; situated 105; space 21, 27; stalled 9

mastery 13, 22, 43–44, 48
measurement: challenges 1, 8; curriculum 20, 64, 78, 93, 109; values 84
memory: long-term 5, 7, 9–10, 26, 30, 34–35; storage 10; working 9–10, 12, 15, 30, 32, 34–35
metacognition 28
metaphor 5, 29, 32, 75
mindset 14
multiplication *see* operations

novices 13–15, 25–26, 30, 69
number/s: consecutive 51, 66–68, 70, 72; decimal 111; even 72; fractional 93; natural 7; odd 67–68, 72; patterns 65; puzzles 65; sequences 64; strings 25, 50, 53–56, 61, 65, 69, 72–73, 127; triangular 126; whole 68, 93

operations: addition 11, 29, 67–68, 126; division 8, 14–15, 42; multiplication 8, 42; subtraction 11, 14–15, 29

pedagogy: critical 92; design 30; folk 123; practice 48
perception 10, 13, 33, 35, 62
play 1, 2, 41, 45, 48, 51–52, 69, 73, 91, 97
prediction 24–25, 27, 34, 56, 60, 70, 83, 99–100, 113–114, 122, 126
problem solving: approaches 2, 44, 46, 50, 89–90; curriculum 42, 124; discrete 42–43; episode 35; integrated 43; mathematical 37, 45, 47, 121; model 47; process 9, 12, 16, 34, 37, 42–43, 47, 77, 83, 124–125; skills 2, 77; types 44

QUACK 44
questioning 37, 45, 54, 66

reasoning 2, 10–12, 19, 21–22, 25, 41–43, 49, 57, 75, 78, 86, 95
relationships 9, 42–43, 50–51, 65, **77**, 81, 92, 98, 127, 129
remediation 14
representation 6–11, 14, 24, 29, 62, 79, 98
robotics 1, 14, 22, 24
RUCSAC 44

scaffold 22, 25, 49–50, 56, 72, 124
schema 5, 7–10, 24–26, 34, 36, 46–47, 72, 108
simile 29
social constructivist theory 11
Stimulated Recall 33
subtraction *see* operations
sustainability 36, 80, 82, 92

taxonomy: Bloom 47, 78; Schulman 123
thinking: conceptual 44; creative 57; critical 20, 106, 115; differences in 5, 22, 36; higher order 7, 47, 90–91; imaginative 41; process of 10, 14, 19, 36, 43, 45, 106
typology 2, 22, 36–37, 48, 54–55, 68, 70–72, 76, 82

visual arts 11

Zone of Proximal Development 26